Purbeck Walks

21 fully detailed country walks of moderate length along public rights of way, in and around the Isle of Purbeck in Dorset

by Rodney Legg

dpc

DORSET PUBLISHING COMPANY
KNOCK-NA-CRE MILBORNE PORT
SHERBORNE DORSET DT9 5HJ

Also by Rodney Legg

Purbeck Island
Ghosts of Dorset Devon and Somerset
Editor *Steep Holm – a case history in the study of ecology*
Monumenta Britannica with John Fowles
Exploring Ancient Wiltshire with George Osborn
Old Portland with Jean M Edwards
Romans in Britain
Purbeck Walks
Old Swanage
The Dorset Walk with Ron Dacombe, Colin Graham
The Stonehenge Antiquaries
Guide to Purbeck Coast and Shipwreck
Hardy Country Walks
Blandford Forum Guide
Lulworth and Tyneham Revisited
Walks in West Dorset
National Trust Dorset

Publishing details. First published 1983.

International standard book number (ISBN) 0 902129 47 3.
Trade sales distribution by Dorset Publishing Company from Knock-na-cre, Milborne Port, Sherborne, Dorset DT9 5HJ, telephone 0963 32583.

Printing credits Main typesetting by Jackie Sugg of Typecast (Photosetting) Yeovil Somerset. Printed by M &T Print in the Old National School Wincanton Somerset.

PURBECK WALKS

Contents

Introduction

THE SCENERY in Purbeck is superb. For dramatic variety of coastline and landscape you will not find better walking country anywhere. Neither can it be matched for the combination of attractions, of spectacular cliffs and nature reserves of international importance, in a land of stone, clay and shale that has had intrinsic value to man from prehistory to the coming of the oil-rigs.

These walks are all on public rights of way and they are all circular routes; that is they bring you back to your starting point. Some are coastal and others inland, but most are a mixture of both.

They were all researched and walked by me for readers of the Dorset County Magazine and have been revised and adapted into this comprehensive batch. It covers all of the Isle of Purbeck that can be sampled through a circuit of public paths – though that sadly leaves out isolated places like Shipstal Point at Arne, which is only reached by a single cul-de-sac right of way. Neither is the 638-feet vulcano-shaped mass of heathland known as Creech Barrow Hill here to be enjoyed. Until a review of Dorset rights of way drags to a close in 1984, and then supposing a positive decision, it is omitted from the county's map of definitive public paths. For legal reasons this has to be the crucial criteria – I can only invite you to walk public paths.

These walks have been tailored to public demand. It was made quite clear that the unsilent majority does not wish to indulge in long treks. Not for the average Dorset Magazine reader could it be a yomp from San Charmouth to Port Swanage. The average length of these walks is of moderate proportions – only some five miles – though here and there I will punish you with a few stiff climbs. A few extend up to eight miles, but many are a civilised four. Anything relevant is mentioned, from the history you stumble across to the hideous asbestos barns that are so useful as landmarks, and the location of strategic snacks.

I give the mileage of each walk but the Countryside Commission guideline is to allow at least an additional twenty-five per cent to such estimates to allow for inevitable meanderings and the impossibility of achieving the sort of approximation to a straight line that you might manage on a pavement. In all there are more than a hundred miles of Purbeck paths walked here. You will find the descriptions and sketches are completely adequate without further aids, though to devise your own variants you will need the 1:25,000 scale Outdoor Leisure Map of Purbeck, produced by the Ordnance Survey. It shows rights of way with green lines though, confusingly, untarred County Council maintained unclassified roads – which are also public – are left uncoloured and in some cases omitted. Most of the paths are well defined and easy to follow, and many have been signposted and waymarked over the past decade.

Always take the obvious into account – these walks were generally researched in conditions that were average to good, and described in the state in which I found them. Only you can consider the current weather conditions, and choose your footwear and clothing accordingly. Some meadowland still floods in winter. A path I might have encountered in extreme drought can be very different after the wettest July of the century. Conversely in some years it will remain delightful in January. Another point is that north is always at the top in the sketch maps, as is the custom.

Not only have the walks been checked out again in a wide range of conditions by the author and Dorset Magazine readers, for whose comments he is most grateful, but a user's test report has been received from Arthur Brook of Sherborne. All suggestions are incorporated. Lastly I should thank a multitude for the pressure from all directions that has led me to this point. In all our Dorset publishing, since 1968, it is the only time that inquiries for a product have been incessant and extended to hundreds of requests. The last straw, characteristically, was that they should be joined by Bill Arnold, my bank manager. He pointed out that here was a clear case of market demand, and added: "Well go on, you know what you've got to do." May he be drawn into sharing a few of them with us.

St Albans Head Dorset

Park considerately.
Take only photographs.
Leave only footprints.
Shut the gates.

— the country code
that doesn't sound
as if it has been
written by a committee

Wool and Coombe Heath

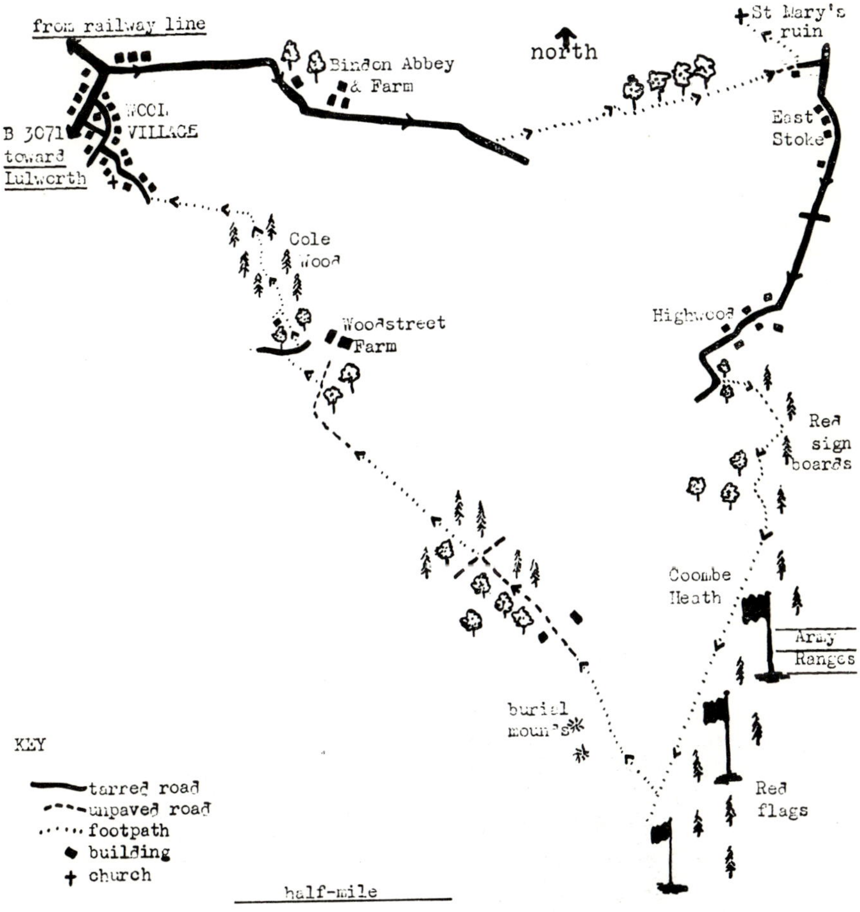

VARIED SCENERY, from meadows and woodland to a great open expanse of wild heath, is covered in this leisurely *seven* mile walk based on Wool village. It explores the little known tract of country between the Frome river and the heathlands on the edge of Purbeck. Mostly the countryside is intimate and undemanding, shrouded in vegetation but crossed by dry paths that do not climb any hills.

On the heath, however, there is a feel of immense spaciousness as the view suddenly opens out to a skyline of the Purbeck Hills. Many of the paths have been waymarked (with direction arrows painted on gate posts and tree trunks). One or two ruins bring touches of historical interest, and if you forget the few well-hidden country retreats, this is today a piece of country that has been largely depopulated.

Park and start in Wool village, which lies between Dorchester and Wareham on the A 352. Leave your car in Spring Street. There is an area of gravel opposite the Black Bear public house, and other parking spaces a short distance to the south at the Cross.

Walk back to the High Street and turn right along it, in the direction of the railway line. At the corner you turn right, where the signpost points to "Bindon Abbey, West Holme, East Holme". This is Bindon Lane, and you pass the village pound. Bindon Abbey is in a quarter of a mile, behind the trees after the road bends to the right. It has the most beautiful setting of any of the monastic ruins in Dorset, with a well preserved layout, stone coffins, and the monks' fishponds — beside a splendid backdrop of trees. For a number of years it has been open to the public, but the day we researched the walk a notice said 'closed', so be prepared for disappointment.

After Bindon Farm there is a straight section of road to the next corner. Having walked around this corner you continue for about a hundred yards and then turn left through the second metal gate, the one that is facing you. Follow the lefthand hedgerow to the end of the field. Pass through the gap in the hedge and then turn abruptly right again after a few yards, through a metal gate. You turn left on entering this field, keeping a boggy oakwood to your left. At the end of this field there is a stile and a plank bridge, and you continue straight ahead, following the side of the wood. You continue to follow the wood beside the edge of the third field as well. At the end of the Long Copse there is a glimpse of the Frome between its reed beds.

The path leaves the field in the extreme left-hand corner (not along the track that runs to the farmyard). In the corner there are two posts marked with yellow paint. You then continue straight ahead across the meadow, keeping the river further over to your left, and follow the line of three oak trees. A second right-of-way branches off to the left to the church ruin. It is in a thicket of dead elms, just before you reach the river. Among the ruined table tombs are a couple of 15th century walls of the old church of St Mary, all that was left after demolition in 1828. Also in this plot is one of the homely gravestones of Dorset, worth quoting in full along with its occasional long 's'. The place is not of the scale of Bindon Abbey, but it does have atmosphere, and is perhaps a little nearer reality for most of us.

To the Memory of
ROBERT CHISMAN
A good Carter, a Faithful Servant
and an honest Man
He ferved as Carter on
East Holme Farm thirty fix years
under five fuccefsive Masters
to the entire fatisfaction of each
Died July 21st:
in the year of our Lord 1822
Aged 52 Years.

After you have explored the churchyard, walk back across the meadow to rejoin the original path. It leaves the meadows at the right-hand side of the Freshwater Biological Laboratories, in the corner by the hedge, and leaves via their drive. This brings you to a tarred road.

Turn right along the road and follow it through East Stoke. You come to a crossroads and continue straight

Gothic style gateway to Bindon Abbey, built in 1797 Photograph: Frederick G Masters

over, along the "No through road". This is signposted to "Highwood 1". It is a leafy lane, with a scattering of expensive homes, at the edge of the heath. The last house you pass, on the left, is Highwood Ferris.

About 200 yards after this house, beyond the first corner, there is a sharp double bend. On the other side of the bends is a straight stretch of road (which leads to Highwood Farm).

On the final part of the bend, by some scrubby trees next to a field, you turn left. One of the trees has a blue arrow painted on its trunk, to the left of a railway-sleeper gatepost. Walk along this track through the wood. You pass a red "Danger Unexploded Shells Keep Out" notice, but that refers to the army ranges which begin on the other side of the fence. The public path is safely on the civilian side, and even if you hear firing there is no need to worry as it will be from tanks half a mile to the left, and they aim towards the sea (not towards you!). Keep the army's fence immediately to your left. You pass some gorse bushes but after that the path is open and comfortable. You walk beside a field and then follow its corner around to the right, still keeping the army's fir trees to your left.

The public bridleway runs beside a very burrowed bank and keeps following the army's fence, first taking a turn to the left and then one to the right, and brings you into an area of old birch woodland. Whoever owns the shooting has gone to the trouble of erecting two deer hides. At the next turn the path goes left again, across a ditch, and still follows the army boundary. Follow the red military signs, and blue waymark arrows.

You come out of the bushes on to a great area of heather. The path still follows the red flags, and take care not to trample the ground as the moister parts have dozens of tiny, reddish, insect-eating sundews. Each leaf is covered with miniature, sticky droplets. This is Coombe Heath, one of the last unspoilt vestiges of Dorset's once endless heathlands, and it still has no buildings in sight. You have instead a fine view of the Iron Age hill-fort of Flower's Barrow, and the line of the Purbeck Hills leftward to Creech Barrow.

Half a mile across the heath, two hundred yards before the third red flag, you turn sharply right at ninety degrees, and walk across the centre of the health. You pass a hundred yards or so to the right of two bracken-covered Bronze Age burial mounds. One, about ten feet high and sixty feet in diameter, is perhaps the finest preserved heathland 'bell' barrow in Dorset. It still has a well marked ditch, five feet wide, around its base, and there is no sign of the centre ever having been disturbed by Victorian diggers.

On the edge of the heath, by the trees, are two cottages. They are about 150 yards apart, and the path passes between them. It runs beside a short stretch of old hedgerow, and then becomes a gravel track leading straight ahead into the woods, crossing a stream. In about a third of a mile you come to a clearing where the main path bends to the right.

Here you continue straight ahead, along a grassy path signposted "Bridleway, Woodstreet ½". You ignore the other bridleway sign as that points to Kimbert's End. Look out for deer. The path climbs the hill and then passes between two old hedgerows, before descending as a sandy track to Woodstreet. Just before it reaches the farm it bends to the right.

As the farm buildings come into sight you turn left, through an iron gate. Follow the lefthand hedgerow across a small field.

On the other side you turn right along a tarred road for about thirty paces and then turn left. A sign says: "Footpath, Wool church ¾". This path passes through a copse, with badger earths nearby. At the top of the slope, a collapsing cottage of stone and thatch can be seen to the left.

The track itself bends to the right, beside a Forestry Commission sign, and then leftwards, following the yellow arrows. This is Cole Wood, and the track emerges from its lowest corner, the closest point to Wool. The route is clearly marked with yellow arrows, and you have to make sure you keep following them.

On going through the gate into the field you turn left, and follow the lefthand hedgerow. It brings you to a tarred lane, a short distance from Wool church.

You turn right, and walk downhill, passing the church. The interior was heavily restored during the last century, which destroyed most of its fittings, but there are three rather large bells on the floor. The oldest is by Thomas Hey, 1350. It still rings to a tap from a metal pen. At the bottom of the lane, opposite the newly renovated Poorhouse Barn, you turn right. This is Spring Street, and your car is only a short distance away. ●

Bindon Abbey's seal

Coombe Keynes eastwards

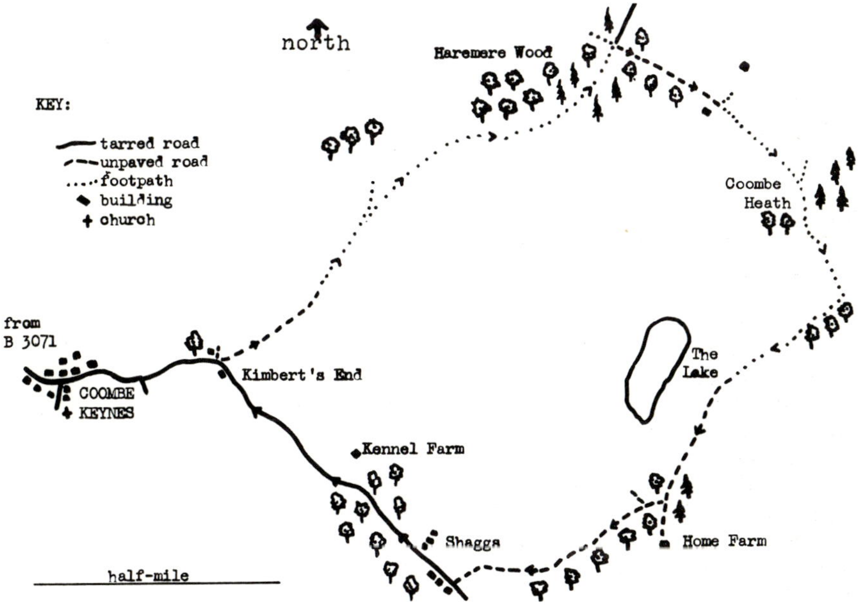

THIS IS a short walk, only *four* miles, intended to round off the afternoon for visitors to Coombe Keynes. It is a pleasant cluster of rural charms. In the 1970s its decline was reversed by three major initiatives – the mediaeval church of the Holy Rood was bought by the villagers who established the Coombe Keynes Trust; derelict cottages have been restored; redundant barns have been converted to homes. Coombe Keynes lies between Wool and Lulworth Camp, and is signposted from the B 3071. The walk explores the countryside of small woods at the fringe of the Purbeck heaths, and gives you a glimpse of the little known lakeland that is one of the gems of the Lulworth estate.

Park and start in Coombe Keynes village. There is limited parking here, beside the telephone box and in a couple of gravel laybys beside the road. Another parking space is on the grass verge on the left side of the road about 200 yards after the end of the village. Make sure you do not block any entrance. In case of difficulty turn back towards the main road. There is a small layby on the left, near the road junction, and if all else fails you can pull on to the verge beside the main road.

Explore the village first. The church is beside the lane that branches off to the right from the village green.

Walk back to the green and leave the village along its principal road, that is with your back towards the

main road, in the direction of East Lulworth. Walk past East Farm and its barns and then out of the village along the lane. This climbs through a deep cutting, overhung by oak and holly, and you pass an attractive thatched cottage tucked away at the brow of the hill. On the other side of the brow you pass a tiled cottage, at Kimberts End, and come to an Army Ranges notice board.

Turn left here, along a rough track signposted: "Bridleway Highwood 1." The first section is between fences, and the next crosses a field. At the centre there is a parting of tractor-ways and you continue straight ahead, towards the wood on the skyline. The track bends a little to the right and passes the right-hand edge of Haremere Wood. The view to the right opens out across the heath to the line of the Purbeck Hills.

You then go through a wooden gate into a plantation. Please ensure the gate is kept shut, on its chain, as the notice asks. In the middle of the wood you come to the end of a tarred road and three wooden signposts.

Turn right, following the pointer: "Bridleway Shaggs 1¾." This gravel track passes Coombe Heath Cottage and emerges on the heath. Continue straight ahead, along a track of rushy grass, which after about 50 yards disappears into the heather.

Walk across the heath, aiming for a point to the right of the army's nearest red flag. You pass to the right of a peat bog, which is floristically interesting. You can now see the line of the Purbeck Hills from Creech Barrow to Flower's Barrow, the hill-fort above Worbarrow Bay.

There is a distinct horse-track across the heath and it bends to the right as you approach the army range boundary. Walk along it, gradually downhill, into an area of birch scrubland. One of the larger trees has a leftward direction pointer and you follow the path into a straight double-hedged trackway.

After the straight section the track bends to the right and you pass some large oaks. After the trees there is a metal gate and the track continues straight ahead, wider and firmer. In about a hundred yards,

The Lake, Coombe Keynes — but you have to admire from a distance

Courtesy: Dorset County Magazine

make sure you stop at another gate and glance over it, to your right. You'll see the waters of the Lake, a large stretch of water edged by trees about 200 yards off. This is as close as the public path network comes to it. On the other side of the water there are reed beds and a stone boat-house with battlements.

The track leads you into a plantation, towards a farmyard, but you turn right about 50 yards after the first clump of beech trees. Blue arrows show the course of the bridleway, which skirts the side of the wood and runs in a straight line. It then turns towards the group of council-built homes at Shaggs.

Turn right at the tarred road, and walk along the lane to Coombe Keynes. It is about a mile. ●

Coombe Keynes church and its font, drawn by Thomas Hardy, who played an active part in the 1860 restoration of the building.

Photographs: National Monuments Record
Drawing: courtesy Hardy Collection Trustees, Dorset County Museum

PURBECK WALKS 3

Lulworth and Durdle Door

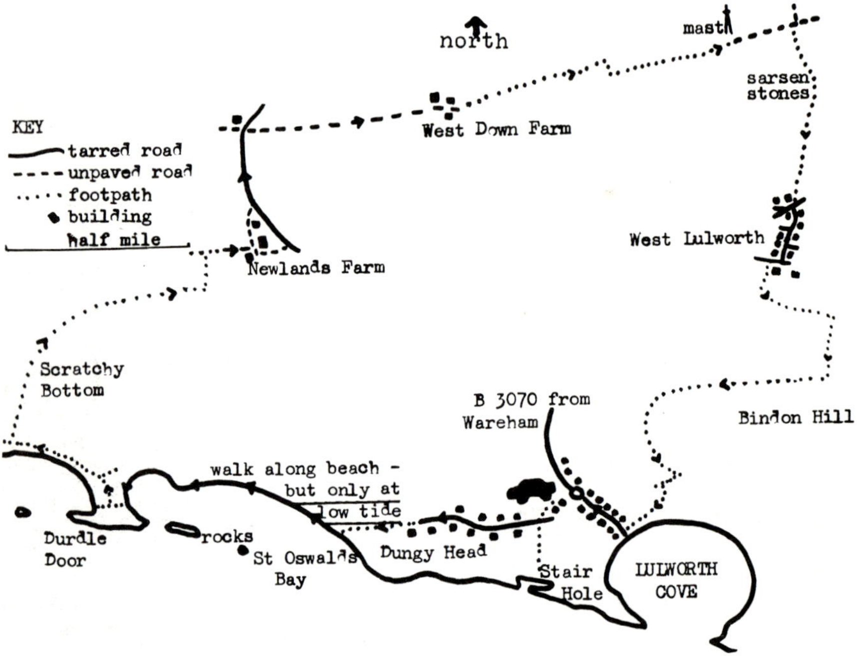

FROM LULWORTH Cove there is a *five* mile walk – that has the variety that is the essence of this famous coastal land-scape, together with the major honeypots – Stair Hole, Durdle Door, and Lulworth Cove itself. The walk takes you into the hills above the village and there are fine views of Portland, the Frome valley, and Purbeck.

Park and start in the main car park at Lulworth Cove. The entrance to this is from the turning circle by the Cove House Inn, at the end of the B 3070 road, five miles from Wareham.

Follow the "Stair Hole" signpost, immediately beside the pay kiosk where you enter the car park. A gravel track skirts the edge of the car park, crosses a tarred drive, and brings you to a grass slope leading up to the cliff edge. From here you can look down on Stair Hole, where the sea has broken through the Purbeck limestone and created two rock arches, as well as a larger broken opening. It is a re-creation of another Lulworth Cove, so far in miniature.

After you've seen Stair Hole, walk back to the tarred driveway, and turn left along it. You climb through Lulworth's most desirable residential area, to the highest houses, Weston and Oswald. The latter is tucked away in a hollow beneath Dungy Head, and a public path passes to its right.

This track descends to the beach at St

Oswald's Bay and you turn to the right, along the shore. If you come to the beach at an exceptional time — and find a very high tide, or stormy seas driving on to it — then don't proceed along it. Instead, climb back up the cliff and turn left towards the top, following the fence line up to the main footpath on the skyline at Hambury Tout. If come into another mini-cove.

Leave this bay at the far end, avoiding another exit path which has land-slipped. The track at the end should be firm, and joins a flight of steps which take you down the other side to the beach at Durdle Door. After you have seen the rock arch, climb up the steps to the top of the main cliff.

The descent into St Oswald's Bay

Courtesy: Dorset County Magazine

you do walk the beach, you'll find the shingle is some of the finest in Dorset, of fish-tank quality. The beach is re-united with the footpath system at the far end of St Oswald's Bay. On the way you get a practical geology lesson, the most important part of the Lulworth story, though it's something the school parties generally miss. Having broken through the limestone barrier (leaving isolated rocks in the bay) the storm-force seas reach the foot of the cliff and leave solution holes, ranging in size from fist-shape to a walk-in cave. As the beach is able to protect the base of the cliff from ordinary tides, this process is reasonably slow. You can test the weakness of the chalk rock with your finger nail. Every three feet there is a band of flints. On the other side of a limestone shelf you

Turn left at the clifftop and follow the cliff path, overlooking Durdle Door and the sea to Portland. The offshore rock is called the Bull. You then descend into a deep-cut dry valley, known as Scratchy Bottom.

Turn right at the bottom of the valley, over a stile. Follow the fence to the head of the valley. You cross two further stiles and go through a gate, to emerge at the Durdle Door caravan camp. The track skirts around the edge of a field.

Turn right at the top corner, along a dirt track. You pass Newlands Farm, the slate-roofed building on the right, which was the favourite holiday haunt of philosopher Bertrand Russell. The farmyard is facing you.

Turn left here and walk up the stony track to the tarred road. Turn left and

walk downhill for about 150 yards. Turn right at the telegraph poles, along the track to West Down Farm. The unmade road is sheltered by a windswept hawthorn hedge. The farmhouse overlooks a prairie, which just about reaches the front door. Continue straight ahead, passing the barns, and follow the dirt track beside the hedgerow.

At the end of the next field you turn right, through an iron gate, and then left across the corner of another arable field. There is a larger metal gate facing you. Go through this, on to a grass track. The Purbeck Hills and St Alban's Head are on the skyline. The track passes the radio mast for Lulworth Camp, and from here the green lane is metalled. In about 150 yards you come to an electricity pole.

Turn right here, into the field, and follow the hedge downhill. You are now heading towards the tank range radar apparatus, on the hill on the other side of the valley. You pass an interesting grouping of six sarsen boulders, with traces of a mound leading westwards from them. We have no record of a prehistoric burial chamber being recorded here, so perhaps some archaeologist could look at them and express an opinion. There are two other sarsen stones in the hedgerow, either side of the stile at the bottom of the field. There is another stile halfway down the hill and you descend into West Lulworth, beside the police house.

Cross the road, into Farm Lane. You pass the village telephone exchange, and a tasteful conversion of West Lulworth Farmhouse barns into holiday cottages. Pass the junction with Shepherd's Way and continue to the end of the road.

Here you turn right, passing the thatched Linden Lea, and turn left immediately after its garage. A track climbs the slope. Turn left at the stile, following the edge of the field. At the corner you follow the field around to the right and walk beside the hedgerow to the top of the ridge. The upper part is pasture land at the edge of the army's tank firing ranges. At the top

Opposite: Durdle Door, with Portland beyond Photograph: Rodney Legg

Nostalgic reminder of steamers at Lulworth Courtesy: Dorset County Magazine

there is a ditch and a bank, built by colonists from Gaul at the start of the Iron Age. Turn right and follow the bank, which conveniently has a public footpath along its length. It would originally have been palisaded, as a timbered rampart. You pass an associated dyke, into the earliest part of the settlement. Continue straight ahead, towards Hambury Tout and Weymouth. The bank gradually curves around the top of the hill, to overlook the Cove anchorage. It protected the eastern shore of the Cove from any landward approach.

Turn right at the cliffside fence and cross the stile. Walk downhill, aiming for the fisherman's boat yard. The notice says "Persons using this path do so at their own risk. No liability accepted by owner or council." That applies to all highways in this country. The notice arises here because Environment Secretary Michael Heseltine intervened to refuse the council permission to close this highly attractive path. It does not seem to be slipping into the sea in 1981, but be careful if it does in the future (there is an alternative descent into Lulworth about 500 yards inland). In early summer this cliff path has masses of a tall and sickly smelling lush green herb. Alexanders, it is called, and thrives in frost-free conditions by the sea.

Turn right at the road at the bottom of the hill and walk uphill, passing the duck pool. After the gift shops you come to the cafeteria and the car park. They provide for tourists in this part of the world and you can look forward to a double cornet of banana ice cream, or you may not. ●

Boatmen and lobster pots beside the Cove, about 1905

Courtesy: Dorset County Magazine

Arish Mell and Fossil Forest

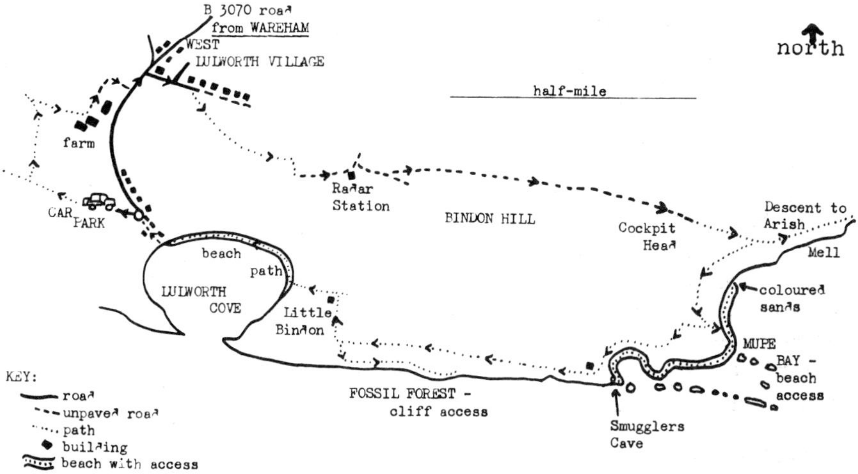

THIS IS a strictly weekend, Saturday or Sunday, walk — for it explores the network of footpaths provided by the army across the western sector of the Lulworth tank gunnery ranges. Generally, these are open each weekend, and there are plenty of signs in the area that announce the position on the day.

However, if you want to make sure in advance, telephone the range office on 0929 462721. The army's "Provisional Firing Programme" is also published weekly in local newspapers. During August, and at the extended holidays of Christmas and Spring bank holiday, the walks are open during weekdays as well.

The walk, covering *five* miles, takes in the spectacular coast scenery at Mupe Bay, and also visits the famous Fossil Forest. The latter has an informative notice-board on site: "Many of the rocks of Purbeck began as sediments accumulating 120 million years ago in swamps. As the soils gradually built up, large pine-like and fern-like trees grew here. Some of these stumps became fossilised, but only the former positions of the stumps, covered by a lime-type deposit, can now be seen. The Fossil Forest is part of a site of special scientific interest. It is an important part of our heritage and deserves your care, consideration and protection."

In other words, the stumps are only the shapes of the trees — not fossilised wood. Geological vandals who attack them with hammers to remove souvenirs take away bits of rock that are no different from the rest of the cliff.

Another point that needs emphasising is that our route has been chosen (at both the beginning and end) to avoid those sections of cliff which suffered landslips in early 1977, and it does not involve you walking any stretches of path which have been closed. Not that this guarantees dryness. Though the army paths are grassy and firm, some on the edges of the range tend to become muddy, and boots should be worn. The cliff slopes are moderate to steep.

Lastly, a reminder. If you enjoy this walk, there is another in the series dealing with the eastern part of the army ranges, from Tyneham to Flower's Barrow. It follows next and is also short, so the pair can fit into a day.

Park and start in the main car park at Lulworth Cove. The entrance is beside the turning circle at the end of the B 3070, the road from Holme Bridge and Wareham.

Leave the car park by the inland path-exit, marked by a stile and gate beside one of the "camping prohibited" signs. Walk along the wide gravel path across this field and go through the gate at the other end.

Immediately you are the other side, turn right. You walk away from the well-marked paths and follow the fence, keeping it directly to your right. This track, between the hillside and a bramble thicket, runs up the valley towards West Lulworth village. At the end of the field the fence bends to the left and you come to a stile.

Cross the stile and then turn abruptly right, following the cattle track downhill into the farmyard. After the barns you turn left, passing Hambury House and sheds.

On reaching the tarred road you turn left for about 50 yards. Then turn right, up a lane marked Sunnyside, beside Cove House. Thirty paces after this road becomes a track called Bindon Road, there is a gate and stile to your right.

Cross this and walk uphill, keeping leftward, so that you climb towards the highest piece of the slope. Towards the summit you come to a grassy bank, and turn left to walk along it. This earthwork follows the side of the hill and marks the site of a timber pallisade erected about 500 BC by some of the first Iron Age immigrants to cross the Channel

Cycad tree stump at the Fossil Forest Photograph: John Pitfield

from France. They used this bank to enclose a square mile of Bindon Hill, giving them undisputed use of both the sheltered anchorage at Lulworth Cove and the east-facing bay at Mupe. You also pass a cross-dyke, running over the top of the hill and giving protection to the colonists' eastern settlements. As you climb there is a sweeping view to the left, over Lulworth Camp, to the power station at Hamworthy.

On reaching the boundary fence of the army lands you turn right and walk up to the mast. Here the notice on the gate should say "Lulworth Range Walks OPEN" if it is a day on which you can continue. Once inside the ranges you are asked to keep between the yellow banded posts — as the army only keeps the paths clear of explosives, and not the rest of the land.

After you have passed the radar compound, continue straight ahead along the chalky track facing you. Fork left along the track signposted "Bindon Hill Walk." You keep on this path for a mile, to the clifftop at Cockpit Head, overlooking Mupe

Arish Mell from Cockpit Head

Photograph: Rodney Legg

Bay. Just as you reach Cockpit Head there is a signpost pointing downhill to the "Coast Path" but you continue straight ahead at this point, aiming towards Worbarrow Tout and the Purbeck bays. Below the next stretch of path there is a steppes-like flatland with the green-brown hulks of more than a dozen tanks, with a whole history of their tracks visible across the plain for nearly a mile.

At Arish Mell you can look, but do not touch. There is no path on to the beach. However, it is worth the effort — if only to look down from the cliff above — for the sea has broken through the chalk escarpment and is slowly eating a new bay into the flatter ground beyond. Lulworth Castle is visible in the trees at the head of the valley.

Turn round and walk back up the slope to the "Coast Path" signpost on Cockpit Head. Turn left, and walk down the steep slope. The actual path at this point starts descending the hill a short distance before you reach the signpost, and it is advisable to take it—you can then see where you are walking, and avoid having to stumble through long grass on the side of a precipice.

At the bottom, just after the "Coast Path" signposts, there is a flight of steps down on to the beach at Mupe Bay. This diversion is completely worthwhile as the army allows unrestricted access to Mupe beach. Its cliffs are multi-coloured sands, with a rock of triangular rocks offshore. To the right, beyond the first line of Mupe Rocks, you come into a second cove. At the far end lies the Smugglers Cave. It is remarkable as it has a false-wall, about eight feet high, built across its back end. This wall encloses a chamber about 15 feet wide by ten feet deep. There are the remains of a door, though this could have been concealed by rocks. The main cave is 40 feet deep.

On walking back to the top, to the signposts, take the left-hand of the two pointers. This path takes you along the clifftop for half a mile to the Fossil Forest. As you pass above the Smugglers Cave you will notice the ruins of a small stone building, about eight feet square, which had its doorway facing the cliff edge and the open sea. A little further on is an interesting wartime pillbox with crinkle-cut walls, resulting from its concrete being poured into corrugated shuttering.

The path down to the Fossil Forest is marked by a signpost: "Please do not damage the remaining fossil trees." The best three trunks are at the extreme eastern end of the ledges, which involves a little minor rock clambering about half-way along. They are hollow at the core and about six feet across. No longer vertical, they tilt with the strata at about 45 degrees towards the mainland. One pair were only growing about ten feet apart.

After walking back up from the Fossil Forest you head inland to the lower of the red flags, and then turn left to leave the army ranges. The chapel cottage, Little Bindon, marks the site of a mediaeval monastery that finally closed down and moved itself to Wool. Resist the temptation to be too inquisitive. On the day we researched the walk a father and his herd of four children had penetrated to the bottom of the cottage garden. This sort of behaviour will provoke people into surrounding their photogenic homes with security fencing.

Walk from the cottage down to the beach at Lulworth Cove, taking care over the last sticky hundred yards, and turn right along the beach. Walk to the Cove café and boathuts. From here a road leads to the car park. One enterprising youngster sometimes sells iron-pyrites as "local fools gold" from a tray on his garden wall. ●

Tyneham and Worbarrow

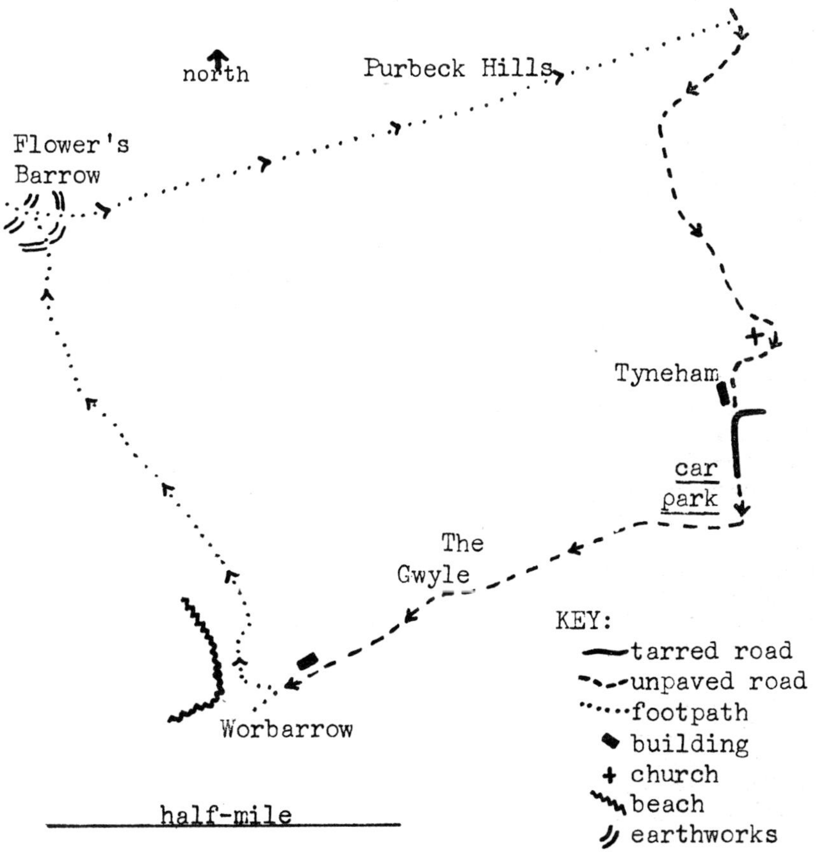

IN WESTERN Purbeck there is a superb *four* mile walk quite unlike any other in this country; the result of a uniquely British compromise which ended the controversy over the public's loss of its rights to enjoy the scenery of the Lulworth tank firing ranges.

For almost every weekend, and during the extended school holidays (at Spring, August and Christmas), Tyneham is the centre for exploring what becomes a massive public park. To make sure it is open on the Saturday or Sunday you choose, either check with the "Provisional Firing Programme" which is published weekly as a public notice by the Dorset newspapers, or phone the army on 0929 462721. Usually there is no problem, and for example this month the walk is open on each of the February weekends.

When this is the case a notice saying "Lulworth Range Walks Open" is put on the army notice boards at Wareham, Corfe Castle and Wool. Apart from one strenuous climb up a hillside, you will find that doing a walk on the Lulworth ranges is less arduous than crossing ordinary farmland. The tracks are well-defined and dry, without any barbed wire blockages, and there is no risk of coming upon a bull. Neither is there any danger of being blown up as the army checks each path for unexploded shells before the weekend starts.

What you have to ensure is that you always keep to the cleared area of the official path. This is marked on the ground by posts banded with yellow paint. Particularly, you are warned never to leave the marked path, nor touch or pick up strange objects, or enter any buildings.

Much of the appeal of tank range walking is that it takes you through a great, spacious landscape that has reverted to the mixed shades of green of an England before there were square fields. It is a sense of freedom that is more than immediate as the views are always expansive and take in rolling downland, distant heaths, and the superb sweep of Dorset's finest coast.

This is why you must make the present access system work. The coloured posts are unobtrusive and deliberately look casual and informal. They simply show the course of the path to which you must keep. The arrangement relies on self-discipline and the alternative would be to encage the paths in corridors of chain-link fencing— and destroy all feeling of exploring wild countryside. Yet that was the original idea, and the present system came about only because amenity groups resisted the army's proposals. So it is up to us to show that unfenced paths function without abuse. On the day we researched the walk we passed about 20 others at various points and the system was working perfectly with the exception of one pair who had unintentionally strayed from the path whilst watching the far horizon, and missed a marker post.

Park and start in Tyneham car park. This is reached from the road which runs along the top of the ridge of the Purbeck Hills between Creech Grange and Lulworth. To find Creech you turn off the A351 Wareham to Corfe Castle main-road at Stoborough. Approaching from this direction, you enter the army

Ghost village of Tyneham Photograph: Rodney Legg

Gad Cliff, above Tyneham valley, and the coast to Kimmeridge and St. Alban's Head
Photograph: Rodney Legg

Sea Cottage in ruin beside Worbarrow Bay Photograph: Rodney Legg

ranges at the summit of Creech Hill. Continue past the sentry post and into the ranges. Half a mile further there is a road which forks off, downhill, to the left. Take this and drive for as far as the road goes, which is into a field marked "Free Car Park", shortly after you pass the ruins of Tyneham village.

Leave the car park by the white painted gate at the south side. This gate is at the point where the tarred road becomes a gravel track. Here the army's colour scheme is lacking, but this is the correct path, and it leads to Worbarrow Bay. The track turns to the right after some stone walls which mark the site of Tyneham Farm. You are now walking beside the Gwyle, a wooded stream-bed which is pungent in spring with the odour of wild garlic. Its other noticeable plant is the stinking iris. Ecologically, the Gwyle has stabilised into something of far greater natural history interest than its managed days before the war. Now the aged trees rot where they die, and enrich the food-chain with limitless insect life, and the gaps they break in the tree canopy lets through light and will in time widen the scope for new plant species. At the end of the Gwyle are the walls and foundations of Worbarrow's fishermen's cottages. The view opens out into one of Dorset's finest seascapes, framed by the conical outline of Worbarrow Tout on the left and with the line of white cliffs from Mupe Rocks and Arish Mell Gap curving round from the right. Out across the bay is the familiar, tilted profile of Portland, and on clear days the lighthouse is visible at the left end, the Victorian convict prison in the middle, and Verne fort at the right. In the foreground, the

Worbarrow Tout and bay Photograph: Rodney Legg

Chalk cliffs westward from Flower's Barrow Photograph: Rodney Legg

rocks of Worbarrow Tout contain the most westerly seam of Purbeck marble, and on the right-hand side of the Tout (just around the first corner) an important geological discovery was made in 1973. Several trackways of tridactyl footprints were found on the surface of a tilted mass of black-speckled limestone. These dinosaur prints are in an "awkward location" on the side of the Tout.

Fork right where a sign says "Warning, Oil on Beach" and walk down to the edge of the shingle. Turn right at the beach, beside the outline of Jack Miller's Sea Cottage, and cross the tiny stream. About 15 paces after the stream there is a wooden post saying "Coast Path" and a stile in the fence. Cross the stile and turn to your left, keeping the cliff fence on your left and the yellow marker posts to your right. The colours of these cliff sands range from brown and white to red and purple. Gradually, the incline becomes steeper and by the time you reach the top of Flower's Barrow you will have risen from sea-level to 550 feet, with views to compensate. Near the top of the slope the path turns to the right and enters the outer defences of the Iron Age hill-fort.

Here you turn right along the path signposted "Whiteway Car Park" but if you have time it is worth turning to the left first along the "Coast Path" to sample the breathtaking prospects of prehistoric life on a cliff-edge. No other major Celtic fort was constructed in a way that incorporates sea cliffs as an impregnable side to the defences. Erosion has since carried much of their settlement over the edge.

Leave the fort along the path signposted "Whiteway" and walk along the summit of the Purbeck Hills. To the left you can see Lulworth Castle and the heathlands of the Frome valley. The track is clearly defined and follows the course of the prehistoric ridgeway, albeit along a line of tank targets as well. A mile after the fort, the track dips and a tarred road comes into view. **You cross a stile at the foot of the dip and then turn right along a flinty track signposted "Tyneham Church and Car Park".** This road descends from the hilltop into the pastoral landscape of Tyneham valley and its outlying farmstead of Baltington. The track skirts around the churchyard of Tyneham's 13th century parish church, and you then walk beside a range of stone-roofed cottages, towards a 1920s concrete phonebox.

Cross the stile and walk out on to the tarred road. Continue straight ahead along the road and walk up the slope into the car park. ●

Tyneham's one preserved building

Photograph: Rodney Legg

Westwards from Kimmeridge

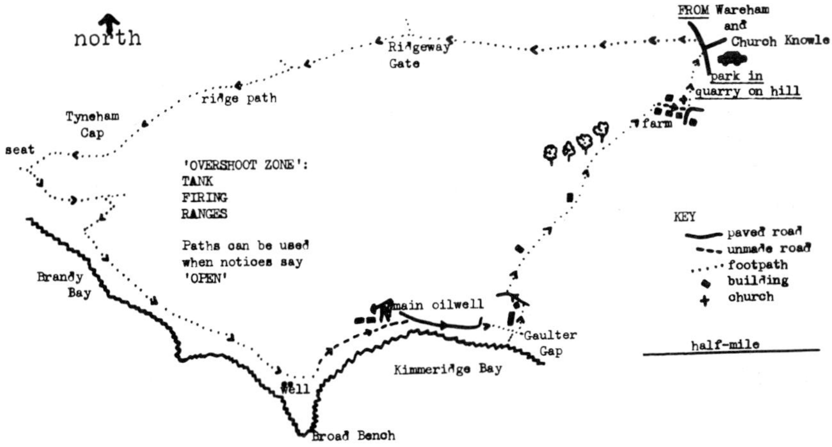

ANOTHER WALK of *five* miles inside the Lulworth Ranges is one of the finest that Purbeck has to offer, and that puts it into the top bracket for scenic quality on national rather than local standards.

It is based on the quarry carpark by the road junction at the top of the hill above Kimmeridge, just before the road drops into the village. This is six miles south of Wareham and three miles south-west from Corfe Castle.

These army paths are open almost every weekend and during the extended school holidays (at Christmas, Spring and August) but to make sure you can check with the "Provisional Firing Programme" which is published weekly as a public notice by the Dorset newspapers. Or phone the range wardens on 0929 462721.

All the paths, on the civilian side of the fence as well, are easy to follow and unobstructed. They are also firm and dry. **Park and start in the quarry at the top of Kimmeridge Hill.** It lies about thirty yards coastwards from the junction at the top of the hill, above Kimmeridge Bay. The quarry has a gravel surface, with space for twenty cars.

Walk back to the junction. There are two path signs, and you take the second (about thirty paces north from the junction) which has a pointer reading "Bridleway Steeple 2" on one side and "Range Walks, Ridge Gate" on the other. Follow the path beside the fence, along the top of the ridge, with Portland lying ahead of you in the distance. On the day we researched this walk there were buzzards soaring on the rising air, caused by a southerly wind meeting the hillside.

Continue to follow the ridge path, straight ahead, in the next field. You come to a flagpole and continue straight ahead if the notice on the gate reads "Lulworth Range Walks Open". This is Ridgeway Gate and inside the ranges you continue straight ahead, still keeping to the top of the ridge, which is now rising and has become the highest point on the skyline. Posts spotted with yellow paint mark the course of the path.

You go through another gate, drop into a slight dip, and climb to the 500 foot summit of Tyneham Cap. The projecting overhang on the next cliffedge is Gad Cliff (shown from below on our cover) which takes its name from the shape of the wedges used by Purbeck quarrymen in splitting stone. Walk down the slope in the direction of this cliff.

Continue straight ahead at the first signpost, keeping the old stone wall to your right. In another hundred yards you come to a second direction post. Here you can smell the sea, and look down to the grey shale cliffs of Brandy Bay, which in smuggling days had the advantage of being one of the few bays on the Dorset coast without a coastguard station, or even a single other building. Beside the guide post a section of the stone wall has been turned into a seat. It is strategically placed, warm and sheltered with a view stretching to St. Aldhelm's Head. The words on the concrete say "1976 J.M.: Jeff'n Ange," plus what looks to be the footprint of their dog.

From here you turn left, towards the Clavel Tower folly, following the "Coast Path" in an easterly direction. At the foot of Tyneham Cap are clumps of stinking iris — misnamed as it has attractions in both smell, flower and seed.

Make sure you turn sharply at this

Gad Cliff from Tyneham Cap

Photograph: Rodney Legg

point. The course of the coast path goes through a half-zigzag here, but the day we undertook the walk a number of people made the mistake of following the track straight ahead.

The path turns towards the wire fence at the top of the cliff. The projection towards the sea, in the middle distance, is Broad Bench. Ledges of shale shelve out into the water. Henbane is amongst the flowers — or seeds — on these cliffs, which fact is noted for the benefit of a naturalist who recently told us he had not seen any growing in Dorset.

The little compound with taps and green pipes in the middle of a strip of concrete is an oil well. The track does not go to the tip of Broad Bench, unfortunately, but bends to the left. A lichen-covered 1940 pillbox to the right is an interesting type, as its concrete was poured into a circular shuttering of corrugated iron. It kept lookout across Kimmeridge Bay. As you come into Kimmeridge, and leave the army ranges, you pass BP's crude oil storage tank, and the mesmerising donkey pump.

Next you walk along a tarred road, but continue straight ahead at the corner, crossing the stile facing you. You pass Gaulter Cottages and a small stream blocked by a tank trap, which if you wish to make a diversion is the access to Kimmeridge beach. The path climbs the steps to the car park.

At this point there is an information board about marine life. Turn left and follow the edge of the scrub to the tarred road. Then turn left again and walk along the road (the "No entry" is for cars) past the public lavatories. You then pass another "Private road" sign and continue for about thirty paces, through the green gate and around the corner, to a metal gate into a field, on the right-hand side.

There is a yellow arrow showing the direction of the footpath, and you follow the right-hand hedgerow across this field. You pass a small barn with a rusting roof, and come to a wooden gate. The seven-foot Purbeck stone

The descent to Broad Bench and Kimmeridge Bay Photograph: Rodney Legg

gatepost it replaces lies in the grass to the left.

Follow the right-hand side of this next field, beside the tiny stream. At the end of this field you cross a stile.

In the next field you follow the left-hand hedgerow, passing a cow-shelter that is built largely of beach rather than quarry stones. You then walk beside a small wood of ash and holm oak. You are now aiming for the barn at Kimmeridge Farm, at the end of the next field.

Beside the barn is a metal gate, and a dirt track leads to the road. The dormer straw holes, built with stone slates in the older barn opposite the farmhouse, is a fine piece of roofing.

At the tarred road you turn left, up the churchyard steps, and the public path continues straight ahead, along the paving stones beside the churchyard wall. The 12th century church, though largely rebuilt in 1872, has a mixture of ancient and Victorian features. In the porch there is an 18th century stone, considered to have been the base of a cheese press. It is two feet long, with drainage channels in the shape of an elaborate CND badge. In the churchyard are coastguards' graves, including one to a young man who "lost his life by accidentally falling over the cliff" and another who drowned.

The path, through the churchyard, continues straight ahead to the gap in the hill on the skyline. The small ruin near the top is the remains of a wall and stone stiles, which might perhaps be adaptable as a seat if Jeff and Ange come this way.

At the top you cross a stile and turn right on to the tarred road. The quarry, and your car, are about forty paces further, on the left. ●

Oil has been pumped from Kimmeridge since 1959 Photograph: Rodney Legg

Eastwards from Kimmeridge

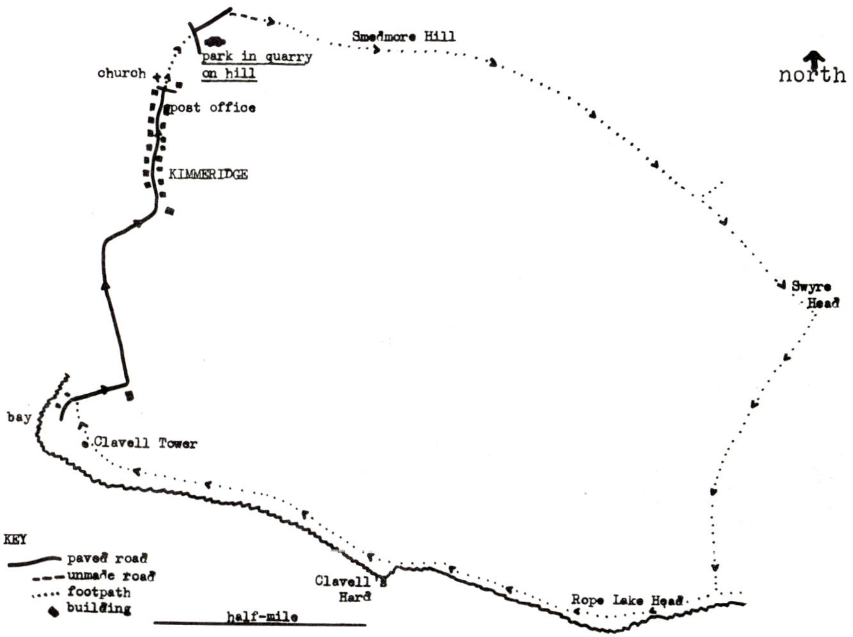

THE CONVENIENT quarry carpark by the road junction at the top of the hill above Kimmeridge – is an ideal starting point for another *five* mile walk. This one goes in the opposite direction, eastwards.

Park and start in the quarry at the top of Kimmeridge Hill. This is six miles south of Wareham and three miles south-west from Corfe Castle. The quarry lies about thirty yards coastwards from the junction at the top of the hill, above Kimmeridge Bay. The quarry has a gravel surface, with space for twenty cars.

Walk back to the junction, and turn right. Walk up the tarred road for about eighty paces and then turn right along a stony track. This goes through an iron gate and climbs uphill. The track runs for over a mile, beside a stone wall at the edge of the ridge, to the prehistoric burial mound at the top of Swyre Head. Here, at 666 feet, you have one of the finest views in Purbeck. It overlooks Encombe house and valley (spot the obelisk on the ridge to the left of the house) and you see Houn's Tout and St Aldhelm's Head in profile.

A signpost beside a stile points you towards the sea, with "Rope Lake Head and Coast Path ¾". Take this path, which was recently made available by agreement: "The path beyond this point is not a public right of way but the owner allows the public to use it

for the time being."

You go downhill, keeping more or less in a straight line towards the sea. There is a stile at the end of the field, and another signpost after the length of dirt track.

At the cliff you turn right. After about a hundred yards the blackstone ledges of grey bituminous shale begin to jut out into the water. The air has that Kimmeridge smell, and it is a mile and a half to the bay.

In half a mile, at Clavell's Hard, you come to the second of three footbridges across small streams. This one — when it is flowing — is worth following, about forty paces to the cliff edge, for one of the best waterfalls in Dorset. It has a drop of about thirty feet. To the right, there is a path that curves down to its base. There, on the other side of the water, is an area of red and yellow rock, about a hundred feet across the top of the outcrop, where the cliff caught fire and burnt for months in 1973. Take a grey bit home and try it on your fire. For the adventurous, at the far end of this ledge the track — which can be slippery — descends to the rocks. Just as it begins to drop, if you look up, you will see a cave a few feet above you. It

Clavell Tower — the cannon has been removed

Quarry car-park at the top of the hill above Kimmeridge

Photographs: Rodney Legg

Purbeck's best waterfall, cascading thirty feet at Clavell's Hard
Photograph: Rodney Legg

was from here that shale was extracted for gas making in the 19th century. The opening is still accessible, and the long, straight gallery is about seven feet wide and seven feet high. Off it, every ten feet (on the west side only at first) are side chambers. But you enter this hole at your own risk, and whether you have a torch is going to depend on whether you have read this page at home first. After about eighty feet it bends and slopes to a lower level. Anyone venturing into these sorts of places should wear a safety helmet, available from a builders' merchants.

Continuing the walk, towards Kimmeridge, you see the bay's two landmarks. The Clavell Tower folly dates from 1831, and the new drilling rig at the oil field, from 1980. When the oil's finally gone, memories of scenes like this will bring waves of nostalgia.

From the folly the path drops down to the bay. If you turn left, towards the coastguard hut, there is an excellent information board, its research by Dr D. P. Brachi. It explains the complex industrial archaeology of the shoreline, some of which will be excavated during this summer.

After you have seen the remains of the stone quays, follow the tarred road, which winds inland to the village. Near the top of the street is the Post Office stores, which stays open at weekends throughout the year. As well as tea and coffee it offers hot pies and a range of light snacks. Places on the coast that stay open for the locals during the winter are deserving of your support.

From the Post Office you continue to the top of the village street, and climb the church steps. You keep walking straight ahead, along the flagstone path beside the church wall.

This path continues into the field and climbs to a gap in the hill on the skyline. Scattered stones near the top mark the remains of a wall and stone stiles.

At the top, after an electricity pole, you cross a stile and turn right on to the tarred road. The quarry, and your car, are about forty paces further, on the left. ●

Opposite: Remains of an 1860 jetty, which shipped the shale from Kimmeridge

Shale mine in the cliff at Clavell's Hard Photographs: Rodney Legg

Bond's Folly and Steeple Leaze

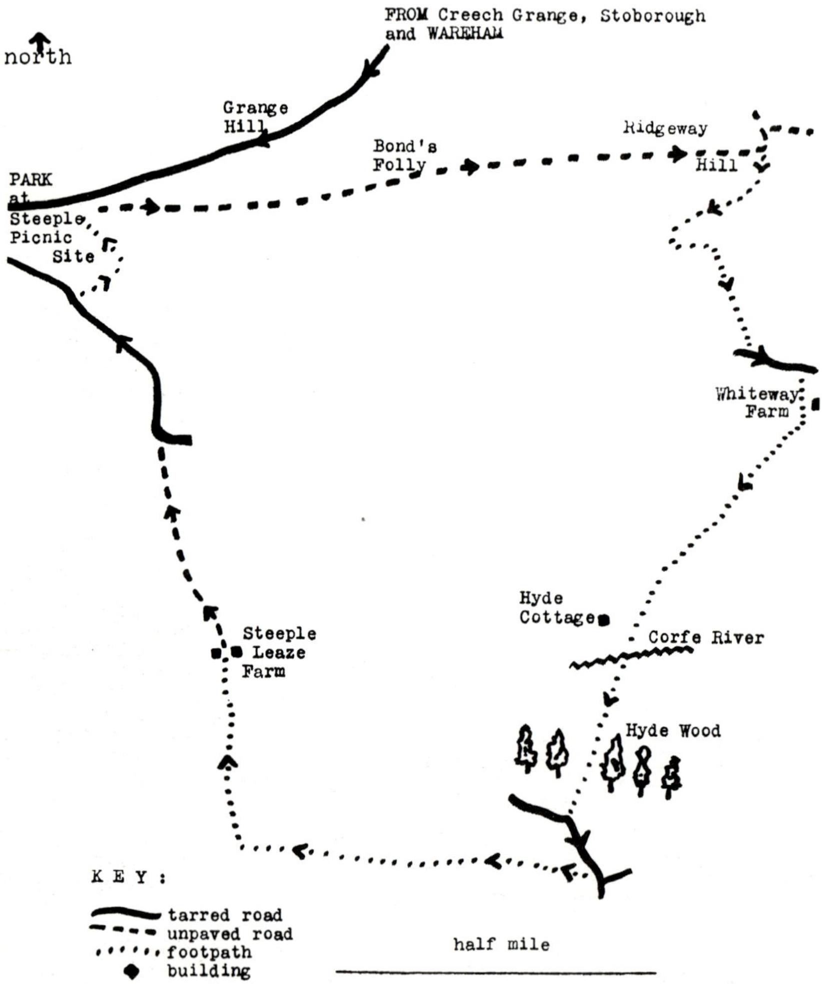

THIS WALK across *five* miles of the chalk and limestone heights of the Purbeck Hills gives constant views of rapidly changing scenery. First you are gazing inland across vast heathlands to the green wedge of the Frome meadows with the foot-hills of the Dorset Downs gathering on the horizon. Next there is the indented shoreline of Poole Harbour on one side of the hill and the valley of the Corfe River and Swanage on the other. Beyond this a coastline panorama opens out to 50 miles wide on a clear day and takes in everything from the Isle of Wight to Portland. Finally, there is a cameo impression of Kimmeridge Bay with its circular tower, a folly, built by Rev. John Richards in 1831. On the other hand, what you enjoy with your eyes has to be paid for by your limbs as there are two steepish hauls before you are back at your car. This is parked in a Dorset County Council public picnic field at the top of Grange Hill. First, you cross the River Frome at Wareham, fork right off the main road by the village pump at Stoborough, and then keep going till you have driven to the top of the Purbeck Hills.

Park and start in the County Council's Steeple Picnic Site on the crest of Creech Hill. Walk out the gate and follow the fence to the right. At the end of the fence, just to the right of a red flag, a track stretches along the hillside for as far as you can see.

Take this. You are walking on Dorset's prehistoric coastal ridgeway, today an open green track across the Purbeck spine. The mass of grey stone on the brow of the hill is Bond's Folly. Its arch stands at 650 feet and encloses Creech Grange in its view. Denis Bond, who lived at the Grange built his folly in the 1740s but has little else to his credit as he was expelled from the House of Commons for land frauds in the Lake District. His folly and an acre of ground are owned by the National Trust.

Continue ahead; only one gate has to be opened, but stop where this track joins another in a T-junction of green lanes at a point overlooked

The valley of the Corfe River at Lutton and Steeple Leaze Photograph: E Dodshon

NEXT PAGE: **The arch of Bond's Folly frames the view into the Frome valley**
Photograph: Rodney Legg

by the bracken-clad summit of Creech Barrow. There is a black-painted iron gate but you must not open this.

Instead, turn sharp right and follow a different path that slopes down the hillside. At the bottom it curves left and then right to follow a hedgerow on to the tarred road.

Turn left and walk downhill to the first gate on the right. Walk through this and you pass beside Whiteway Farm. At the other side of the farm there is a rusty gate. Open this, turn right, and go towards the cattle-trough.

Walk diagonally across the field to the left of the trough. At the opposite corner there is a small bridge across a ditch. Cross this and walk diagonally across the next field.

Halfway along the next hedgerow there is a gap. Walk through and turn to the right. There is a gap about 100 feet along the righthand hedgerow and you duck under some barbed wire into the next field.

Walk diagonally across this field as well, keeping Hyde Cottage on your right, and aim for the third power-line post from the left. Cross the stream in the lower righthand corner of the field. It does not present any real problem (although there is a badger's lavatory to walk through on the opposite bank). Slip under the barbed wire fence at the top of the slope.

Continue ahead to the top righthand corner of the field and walk between the gateposts. Cimb straight up the slope (on which the beds of Purbeck stone are exposed) through the gap of light scrubland that separates Hyde Wood from Beach Coppice.

Ahead, between the first and second poles from the left, there is a wire-gate beside a tarred road. Turn left and walk down to just before another road branches off to the left.

Opposite this, on the right, there is another wire-gate. Open it and follow the top of the escarpment overlooking Kimmeridge Bay. At the end of this long field, near the lefthand corner, are the remains of an old gate. Climb under or over this obstacle and then turn immediately right to follow the stone wall to the end of the field.

Duck under the fence at the post with a yellow painted marker. Continue down the slope through old stone workings and follow the righthand overgrown hedgerow to the farm buildings in the valley. Walk through the yard of Steeple Leaze Farm and straight up the hill ahead.

Turn left at the tarred road and keep walking up the hill. A few feet in front of a white-painted Army gate No. 13, on the right, there is an opening in the hedge and a track up the hill. Follow this and you come out on top of the hill beside your car. ●

Steeple picnic area, above Creech Grange Photograph: Rodney Legg

Corfe's old claylands

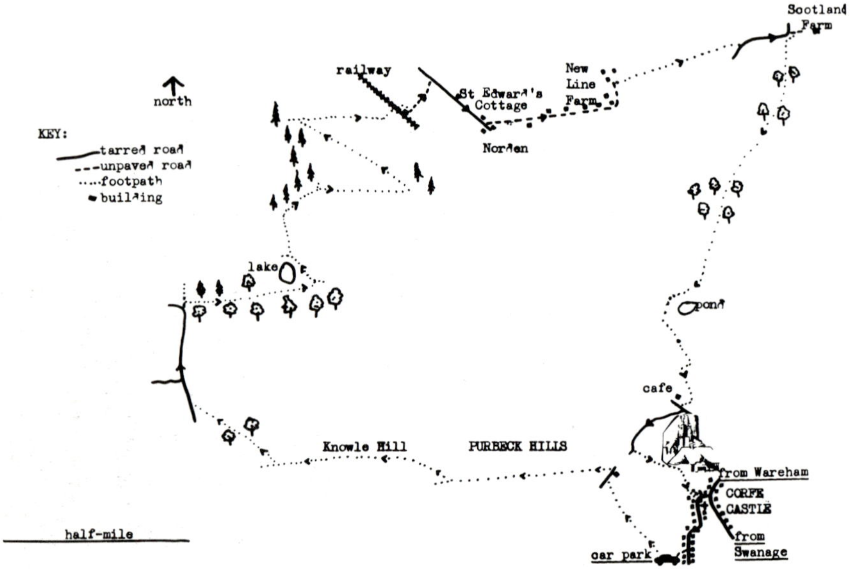

THIS CIRCUIT of *six* miles at the heart of Purbeck takes you through some of its wildest country. Much of the area north of the Purbeck Hills was dug for clay, to feed the Staffordshire potteries, from the beginning of the 19th century. If English China Clays wins its current planning applications then a big new open pit will be gouged from the heath at Norden. Yet the heathland is resilient, and swift-growing vegetation has masked all but the deepest traces of the past. Little is left of the equally great excavations of two decades ago. Only where the water has filled a deep pit is there a direct reminder of an industrial past. But never forget that you are walking on clay. This is a walk for dry days, and if you take it at a wet time of year then put on footwear and clothing appropriate for rough country. The walk starts from Corfe Castle, and crosses both the eastern (common crossing) option for the village by-pass and that of the western (railway wrecking) alternative. This is the last chance to walk Corfe's landscape as it is, and if councillors could be kicked into a little healthy exercise they would realise that any cursed by-pass should go through a tunnel in the hill. Both the present routes are equally deplorable in cutting apart one of the finest settings that this country can offer. Do this walk before it is too late, and think of the disasters that have been caused through history by those who draw lines on maps. Vote with your feet, and see for yourself.

Corfe Castle from the foot of West Hill Photograph: E J Williams

Park and start in the main village car park. It is signposted from the main road – turn into the Square and then left into West Street. The car park is about 400 yards along West Street, on the right-hand side. Park in this car park.

About 80 yards from the entrance hut there is a stile with a footpath marker beside an electricity transformer pole. Walk across the centre of this field to a concrete footbridge on the other side. This crosses the Corfe River. On the other side you walk ahead just right of centre, towards the ash trees against the skyline. On the other side of a bridge of railway sleepers you walk uphill, with the castle and village now to your right.

Head towards the right-hand end of the main hill in front of you. A scrubby embankment to your left is an encampment known as the Rings. It is a siege work of the 12th century, constructed by King Stephen who failed to capture the castle in 1139. It came with the castle itself into National Trust ownership in 1982.

The path brings you to the tarred road at the foot of the escarpment. Turn right and walk down the road for 80 yards. There is an iron gate on the other side, opposite the entrance to the bungalow. It is signposted: "Bridleway, Bare Cross $1\frac{3}{4}$".

Follow this track, which skirts the left-hand edge of the hill. It runs between a barbed wire fence and the hillside for about a third of a mile. The main track then bends to your right, uphill, but you continue straight ahead, following the fence. You then go through a wooden gate and continue to walk between the fence and the foot of the hill. Just before the end of this field you fork right, uphill, to an iron gate on the skyline.

Follow this track to the top. Continue to keep the fence to your left and pass a

You sample Purbeck's lake-land for free, though this gem is at a price — Blue Pool
Photograph: Rodney Legg

couple of Bronze Age burial mounds. This is Knowle Hill and you are overlooking the valley from Church Knowle to Tyneham. At the end of the field there is a gate and stile.

There is also a gate and stile at the end of the next field. Creech Barrow Hill, bracken covered, appears on the skyline and you then have a view over Wareham and Poole Harbour.

As you approach the next rise, the English China Clays chalk quarry at Cocknowle comes into view – as soon as you spot this you turn sharply right and descend the north side of the hill to a stile in the fence. It is next to a gorse clump and as you approach it from the hill there is a view of Wareham directly behind it.

Head downhill, aiming for the pair of road junctions below. There is a path down the slope, through the gorse, which comes out in the trees at the foot. If, however, you stray from this you can find it again at the bottom, by entering the area of hazel scrub and walking along the fence until you find a stile, which was in pieces in 1982.

This brings you into a field and you walk straight across the centre to a metal gate on the other side. You come on to the tarred road at its junction with an unmade track.

Turn right, and continue straight ahead at the road junction, following the sign to: "Furzebrook, Stoborough, Wareham". Walk along the lane for about a quarter of a mile. The road then bends to the left, at the hazard chevrons.

Here you continue straight ahead, towards the plantation, but only for about fifteen paces. Then you turn sharply right, along a track beside an old oak hedgerow that has now grown into bent trees. In about 250 yards you come to two estate boundary stones, like miniature grave stones, placed back to back. The west-facing one reads "T.B." and the east one "A.P. Sept 1910". In about 200 yards you come to another two stones, this time on the right (with the "A.P." facing north, "T.B." south). Just beyond these, to your left behind a big pine tree, is a large lake. Like the Blue Pool it was a 19th century claypit.

In about a hundred yards you turn abruptly left, along a track that is a stone's throw from the lake, though you have to be tall to see it over the gorse. At the end of the section beside the lake you turn right, along a wider track into more open ground. You then come on to heath-covered moorland with a view across to Poole Harbour and Hamworthy power station. You pass two prehistoric burial mounds. The path then runs beside a length of mesh fencing, and a signpost at the corner points you right along a "Pathway".

You are now heading towards the area between the harbour and the left-hand edge of the hills. Walk across to the scrub and trees on the other side of the open moorland.

You now turn sharply left, almost back upon yourself, and head for the right-hand end of the pine wood on the skyline (the right-hand edge of the wood which has the "Pathway" sign). As you get near it the edge of the wood seems indistinct, but in the trees there is a tall mesh fence. Keep it immediately to your left, and a well worn trackway leads to the corner of the wood. Here there is a junction of sandy paths.

Turn right, keeping a barbed wire fence and scrubby grassland to your left. Hamworthy power station becomes visible. The track brings you to a pair of white gates across the railway. This is the extremity of the Purbeck line these days, a siding from the clay works and oil terminal. You are now walking towards the sound of the traffic, and come to a modern dormered farmhouse. Turn left and walk

along the track to the main road.
Here you turn right, and walk along the verge for a quarter of a mile. You pass St Edward's Cottage. About 200 yards after this cottage, opposite a postbox and Catseye Cottage, there is an unmade road.
Turn left along this road, beside the house named Picardy. At the end of the road is New Line Farm (preserving the name of Dorset's first railway, a clay tramway of 1805). As you come to the barns you turn off the concrete road to the right, along a muddy track. Corfe Castle is now visible, silhouetted to your right in a view that shows the gap between the hills.
The farm track joins a tarred road and you continue straight ahead along it, for about 300 yards, to the corner with the farmyard. Go through the iron gate facing you and then immediately right again, into the field that lies beside the corner. Then turn left, at a silver birch tree with a footpath marker, and keep the hedgerow to your left for about fifty yards. Then continue straight across the heath, keeping the birch scrub to your left. After about a hundred yards from the start of the scrub you then enter it, passing between holly bushes, into a field surrounded by oaks.
On the other side, near the right-hand corner, there is a break in the holly and boggy land behind. Cross this with care, to a small stream and then a stile on the other side.
From here the castle is in view, and you head towards the end of the hills to the right of it. On the other side of the field there is a yellow footpath marker on a fence post that is a little higher than the rest. Behind it, in the kink in the fence line, is a scotch gate.
The path is well marked through the ivy-clad birches, but in about fifty yards the right-of-way continues straight ahead from the main path, and is indicated by an arrow on a tree. From this point you are aiming at the hill to the left of the castle. In the far corner of the wood there is a stile into the field.
From here you head towards the end of the hill to the left of the castle. This brings you to a stile into some scrub-land. Follow the fence uphill beside the bracken. You pass a flooded clay working.
As you come to the two electricity power lines the track bends to the left. You are now heading towards the gap between the hill and the castle. At the top of this clay spoil heap you turn right, towards the hill to the right of the castle. The track then descends towards the castle keep.
You then walk beside the railway fence, to a stile into a field. Continue to keep the railway to your right. In about 150 yards you cross the railway trackbed by a pair of stiles and then turn left. Follow the railway fence down to the Castle View Cafe, and walk to the main road at the cafe entrance.
Cross the main road at the bridge and take the minor road facing you, between the stream and the castle mound. Just before the next bridge you turn left, along a footpath that continues to follow the foot of the mound. This path brings you into the village square.
Turn right, along West Street, passing the Town Hall Museum and the Fox Inn. The car park is in 400 yards, on the right-hand side of the street. ●

Courtesy: Dorset County Magazine

Farthing token issued by Edward Harvey of Corfe Castle in 1657

Corfe Common and Kingston

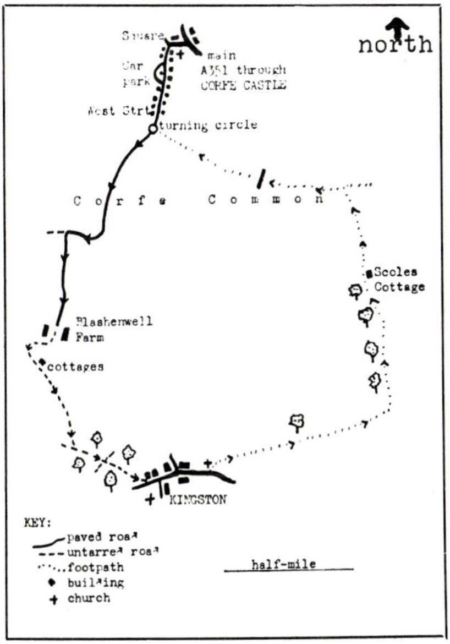

CORFE CASTLE is an ideal starting point for a walk, except during midsummer when severe traffic congestion turns it into a place difficult to enter, leave or even find space in which to park. This *five mile* walk is intended for the off-peak months and strikes off to the south of the village across the common.

Most of the way you are on firm ground but the soil becomes damp at Woodyhyde and tough shoes are needed. Nowhere is there a shortage of visible history, and as with many parts of Purbeck the whole time it can feel like tramping across an ancient monument. Scenically, and for botany and wildlife, the walk is also well above average as it crosses distinct geological boundaries from the Wealden sands and clays into the limestone belt.

Park and start in Corfe Castle village. Turn right off the main A351 road into Corfe Square and then immediately left, by the cross, into West Street. The car park is in about 200 yards, on the right, and costs money.

Walk back to West Street and turn right, walking out of Corfe with your back to the castle ruin. This street has become a cul-de-sac but in mediaeval times it was the main road into Corfe, and along it were dragged sledges carrying Purbeck's entire output of marble. At the end of the road there is a turning circle for cars and you continue straight ahead, through the gate, on to Corfe Common. It came into National Trust ownership, with the Bankes bequest in 1982.

Follow the tarred lane across the common. At the far side you cross a stream and about 70 yards further on there is a gate and cattlegrid.

Continue on the tarred road, beside an area of open grassland looking across the common to the castle, and then follow the road as it bends to the left and climbs gradually uphill towards Blashenwell Farm. The stone tower emerging from the woods on the hillside to the left is Kingdom church, built by the Victorian architect George Street who also designed St. Peter's in the centre of Bournemouth. As you approach Blashenwell Farm there is an exposed cutting on the left, through the cream-coloured tufa deposits which underlie these fields and have over the past 8,000 years covered and preserved entire Mesolithic habitation layers, complete with flints, hut debris, bones and domestic rubbish.

The tarred road ends at a "No entry" sign but this is intended for cars. The public bridleway goes through the farmyard. As you enter the farm walk straight ahead across the concrete yard, keeping the pond and large stone-roofed barn to your left, and walk across to the black painted gate in the far right-hand corner.

A stony track winds uphill, past a pair of cottages, and you follow it uphill for half a mile to the large wood at the top. Halfway between the cottages and the wood there is a gate and on the other side, just to the right, there is an exposed and slanting outcrop of Purbeck stone, about 30 feet across.

At the top, left-hand, end of the field there are two iron gates and you take the left one, into the wood. Follow the stony track. In about a hundred yards you continue straight ahead over a woodland crossroads. You come to a line of eight garages and the track then emerges in Kingston village.

Turn left and walk downhill past the post office and stone pump to the Scott Arms. Here you continue straight ahead at the junction, along the road uphill and signposted to "Worth, Langton, Swanage". The last building in the village is its earlier, redundant 19th century church, behind a high, locked gate. **On the left, immediately after the churchyard wall, there is a wooden gate. Go through this and walk beside the churchyard wall for about 50 paces. There is a second gate in the stone wall facing you. Do not go through this but turn right, keeping this stone wall on your left.** The wall crosses a series of mediaeval strip fields. Five parallel banks, each about 30 feet apart, run at right-angles to the wall you are following, and pass underneath it. Con-

West Street, Corfe, leads to the common, though its users have changed since 1910

Courtesy: Dorset County Magazine

tinue following the wall downhill, to an iron gate in the dip, and go through this. Keep walking ahead, and slip under a wire fence, with the stone wall still on your left and a line of electricity poles now to your right. The track enters a slope strewn with the pits and spoil heaps of mediaeval quarrying. You continue to follow the poles, ignoring openings through the stone wall to your left.

Finally, about half a mile from Kingston, the cable line turns uphill (to the right) and here you walk into the corner of the field. There is an old gateway and you go through this and turn half-left, walking downhill until you meet a stone track.

Follow the stone track for a few yards only, when a muddy track will appear on your left leading through rough ground to a water trough near a wooded gully. Hop over the stone wall at this point and follow the gully downhill through three fields until you see an attractive stone cottage set in a wooded garden.

The path passes through the garden of Scoles Cottage, on the left side of the house. Two gates are provided, the second of which leads on to Corfe Common.

Once on the Common you continue straight ahead, uphill, until you are on the skyline. There is a line of burial mounds and a view of the village and hills.

Turn left along the top of the ridge. You come to an iron gate on to the road.

Cross the road and go through the gate opposite. A notice warns that the haywards will impound any unlicenced animals they find grazing.

Walk straight ahead across the common for about half a mile. The ridge is now on your left and is scarred by more than a dozen deep ruts where stone sledges were tugged over the summit. In places these gouges cut through the field banks of an Iron Age settlement.

Keep close to the edge of the village as you walk across the common and leave by the tarred road. This is the end of West Street, where you started the walk. The quickest way into the car park is through the exit, the first turning on the left after Webbers Close. ●

Corfe Castle and village Photograph: Edward Gearey

Corfe to Houns-tout Cliff

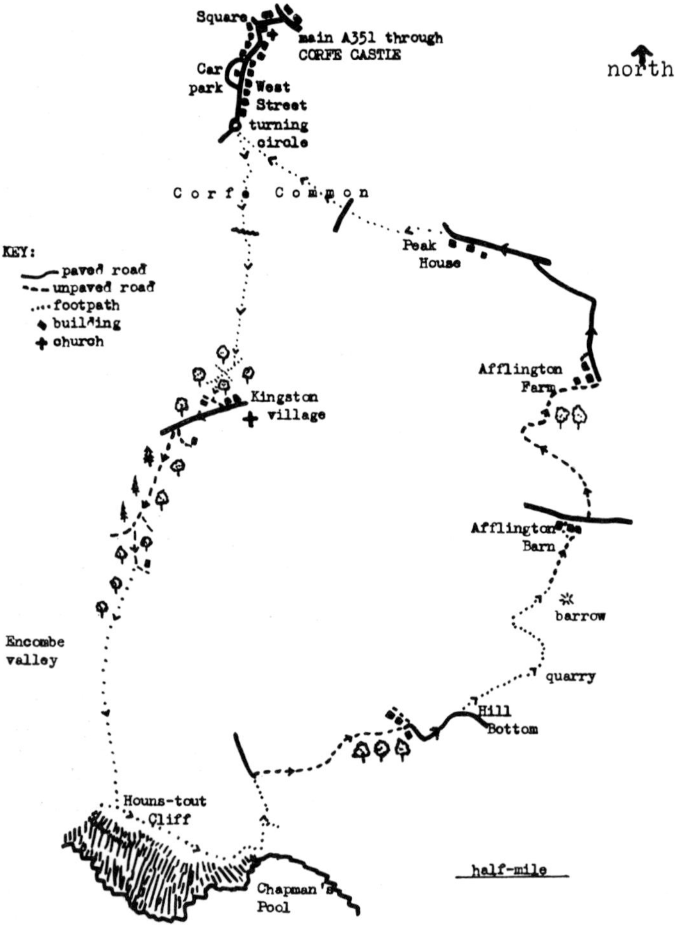

CORFE CASTLE is not only one of Britain's most impressive beauty spots, but provides an excellent starting point for walks rich in both scenery and visible history. This *eight* mile route takes you to the top of one of the highest cliffs on the South Coast, and across distinct zones of geology and vegetation. There is plenty of wild country, including at Hill Bottom and above Afflington some of the finest vestiges of Purbeck's original limestone landscapes. All the paths are well marked, dry and easy to follow. **Park and start in Corfe Castle village. Turn right off the main A351 road into Corfe Square and**

then immediately left, by the cross, into West Street. The car park is in about 200 yards, on the right.

Walk back to West Street and turn right, walking out of Corfe with your back to the castle ruin. This street has become a cul-de-sac but in mediaeval times it was the main road into Corfe. Sledges were dragged along it, carrying Purbeck's entire output of ecclesiastical marble. At the end of the road there is a turning circle for cars and you continue straight ahead, through the gate, on to Corfe Common.

A tarred road leads on to the common. You walk straight ahead, a little left of centre, on to the close-cropped grass. Walk into the common, keeping to the grass between the main clumps of bracken. There is a track that skirts the side of a shallow dip, to the prehistoric burial mounds that are strung along the ridge in the middle of the common. Aim for a point just to the left of the last, right-hand, barrow mound. Then continue downhill, in the general direction of Kingston church tower, on the hilltop facing you.

In the valley, at the end of the common, there is a stile in the blackthorn hedgerow. It has yellow footpath markers. Stone flags bridge the stream and you continue straight ahead across a narrow meadow to a wooden footbridge on the other side. Walk into the middle of this next field, aiming for the cluster of three houses a little left of centre.

You then go into the triangular-shaped far corner of the field, and are now walking directly towards the church tower. There are some churned-up stepping stones and a stile in the corner, leading to a length of double-hedged track, leading uphill. You then go across another stile and follow the left-hand hedgerow, still heading towards the church.

Two more stiles take you straight across a driveway and you pass to the left of a horse-hut. At the top of the slope you cross into the next field and walk up to the transformer box just to the right of the church tower. This field contains the outlines of what seem to be mediaeval cultivation strips, but running across the middle is the grassed-over embankment of a roadway, 18 feet wide and three feet high.

The footpath leaves the field and goes into the trees about 30 feet to the right of the transformer poles. You go through an iron kissing gate and then turn right, uphill, along a dark driveway through the trees.

In a short distance you come to a cross-roads of tracks and continue straight ahead, but only for about another 30 paces. There you turn left into the trees, uphill along a path that runs through the sycamores. You come out on a stony track to the left of a line of eight garages. Turn left along this track for a few yards and walk up to the tarred road.

Here you turn right, for about a hundred yards, uphill to a collection of notices. Turn left along the stony track marked "Private No Entry. Footpath to Hounstout". "Private No Entry" is in this case the local dialect for "Public Footpath". After the straight stretch of track you come to a section of tarred road and fork immediately left, along another track signposted "Footpath to Hounstout". This becomes a grassy farm track above the ash and sycamores of Quarry Wood. A stile brings you on to open limestone downland, with a spectacular view over Encombe valley to the sea.

Walk along the top of the plateau, keeping the stone wall to your left. Follow the wall for a mile to the top of the Houns-tout cliff, 500 feet above Chapman's Pool.

Turn left at the top of the cliff, over a stile, in the direction of Chapman's Pool. You'll notice that you are on higher ground than the coastguard cottages at St Aldhelm's Head. The path descends a rather hairy flight of wooden steps, which we found to be more trip-prone than the untouched hillside. As you approach Chapman's Pool there is a notice saying "Coastal Path Eastwards Closed".

This refers to the track down to the beach at Chapman's Pool, not to your route which is uphill to the arable field (wheat where once cars parked!). A track has been left unploughed and leads inland. On the other side of the field you come to a cattle grid on to a tarred road. Turn right along the track signposted to "Renscombe Fm ¾, Worth 1¼". In half a mile is a tarred road and you come to the cottages of Hill Bottom. This valley echoes to the 'yaffle' of the green woodpecker.

The road bends to the right, downhill, after the first cottage and you then cross a stream. About a hundred yards from the bridge the road begins to bend to the right, to climb up out of the main part of the valley. At the bend you turn left, along a rough track signposted "Bridleway to Afflington Farm 2". This wild valley is Hill Bottom, but the wooden footpath sign is a few feet to the right from the ancient line of the track. You'll find the best pathway a few yards to the left, on the other side of the stream bed. It follows what is left of a collapsed stone wall and brings you in half a mile to the edge of a large open stone quarry.

Fork left here, uphill, along the track signposted "Afflington Barn ¾. Corfe Castle 3¼". At the top end of the valley the bushes are

Chapman's Pool, from Houns-tout

Photograph: Frederick G Masters

white with lime dust and the track then bends to the left, away from the quarry. Near the top of the valley the track bends to the right, through an iron gate, and you climb to the top of the hill. To your right is the Afflington Barrow, which in Victorian times was dug open to reveal a cremation and nine later skeletons.

The track continues straight ahead, beside the stone wall, to the farm buildings at Afflington Barn. Walk to the left of the barns, towards the electricity pole, and cross an iron gate. A track beside the house leads to the tarred road.

Cross over and head downhill, along the stony lane signposted: "Bridleway Afflington Farm ¾". Corfe Castle is now in view. The line of electricity poles follows the track into the valley. It crosses the outcropping of the Purbeck stone beds. Towards the bottom you follow the blue arrow, staying on the main track as it bends to the right, and then to the left through an iron gate. Afflington Farm is at the bottom of the hill.

As you approach the buildings you fork right, alongside the poplar trees. Go through the iron gate and continue to the right of the asbestos barn, making sure that you go round the back of the farm buildings. The dirt track then passes the front of the farmhouse and becomes a tarred road, leading to the railway line and the main road.

Turn left along the main road, for about 200 yards to Peak House, which is on the bend. Here you cross to the left-hand side of the road and go through the gate (marked "Bridleway") on to Corfe Common. Follow the group of barrow mounds, along the ridge across the centre of the common.

Head a little to the right of the last mound before the road. Cross the road to the gate on the other side. A notice warns that the haywards will impound any unlicensed animals they find grazing.

Walk straight ahead across the common for about half a mile. The ridge is now on your left and is scarred by more than a dozen deep ruts where the sledges loaded with stone were tugged over the summit. In places these gouges cut through the field banks of an Iron Age settlement.

Keep close to the edge of the village as you walk across the common and leave by the tarred road. This is the end of West Street, where you started the walk. The quickest way into the car park is through the exit, the first turning on the left after Webbers Close. ●

Limestone landscape: the glen at Hill Bottom Photograph: Rodney Legg

Seacombe and Chapman's Pool

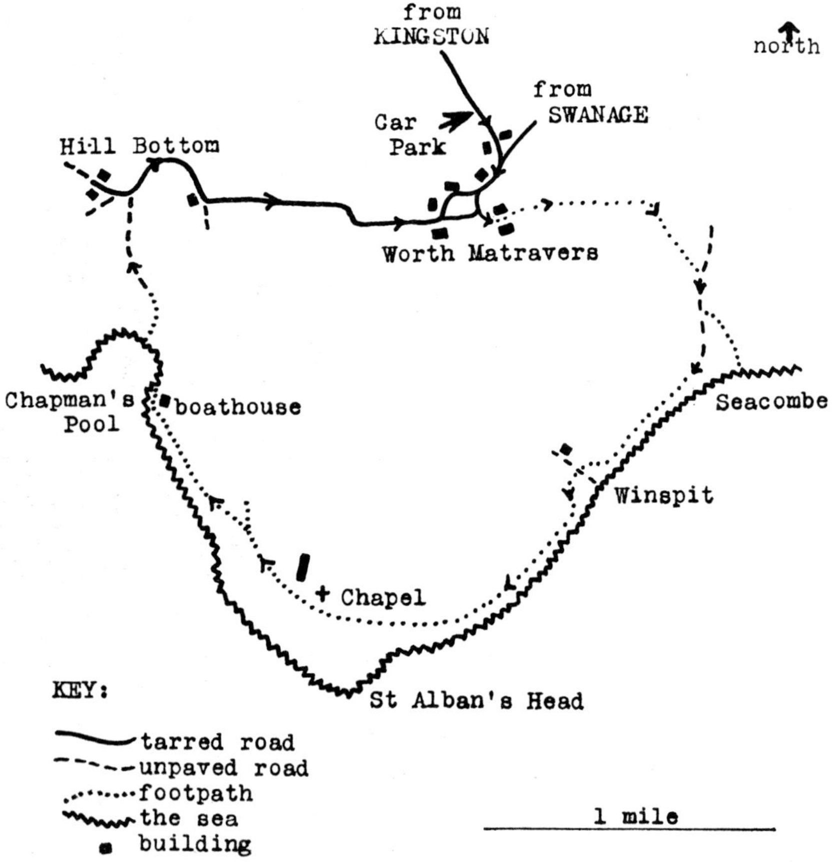

THIS IS ONE of the most beautiful and interesting walks in Dorset; and that is high praise. It is a completely coastal walk and there is a maximum length of clifftop walking with views along the Channel from the Isle of Wight to Portland. The *six* mile route encircles the peninsula of St. Alban's Head which is the southernmost part of rocky Purbeck. There is no worry about where to leave your car. The walk starts from the village of Worth Matravers which lies four miles south of Corfe Castle.

Park in Worth's village car park. It

Coastal valley at Winspit Photograph: Rodney Legg

Edge of the quarry shelf at St Alban's Head Photograph: Frederick G Masters

lies on the Kingston road above the Square and Compasses and there is a fee box. There is also parking space for four cars near the church gate. Go down to the village pond and keep left to where a wooden signpost says: **"Footpath to Seacombe."**

Follow this track sharply left round the first corner. It runs beside a wall above the garden of a house called See-mans. Go straight ahead across the field at the edge of the village. Keep the stone wall on your right and head for the top of the hill. There is a stone stile in the wall which runs across the hilltop. A direction arrow heads you straight across the next field. There is another stile and then you drop down into Seacombe Bottom. This land came into National Trust ownership with the Bankes bequest in 1982.

Pass 'under' the wicket gate at the bottom of the hill. Turn right along the tall hedge of hawthorn trees which follows the remains of an old stone wall. This brings you out on a dirt track and you veer right to follow this up the hill in front.

If you want to go down to Seacombe to see the quarries, carry straight on towards the sea and then double back. These quarries are dangerous and you will see that there have been many rock-falls.

Follow the path out of Seacombe Bottom and on to the western cliff-top. Continue along the cliff path to Winspit where you descend almost to sea-level and then go up the opposite side. Make sure you keep to the cliff edge and skirt the quarries on both sides of the valley. These cliffs are particularly interesting to naturalists and you may find anything from an orchid to a puffin.

Limestone crags of Emmetts Hill

Photograph: Rodney Legg

Boathouse at Chapman's Pool, with Houns-tout Cliff across the water
Photograph: Rodney Legg

In May, when we researched this walk, some of the cliff slopes were mauve with flowering thrift and at one point you could look down on nests of young cormorants.

Carry on to St. Albans Head where you pass the untidy ruins of a wartime wireless station and aim for the coastguard lookout. To the right is the square stone chapel to Aldhelm which was built in the 12th century and is worth a look if you have the time.

Continue along the cliff path to the top of a deep valley. From here you see the sheer cliff of Emmetts Hill with Chapman's Pool beneath and the view along the Dorset coast to Kimmeridge, Lulworth and Portland.

Fork left at the bottom of this valley along the path that takes the undercliff. It looks rough but is easy to follow.

Enter Chapman's Pool by the boathouse and walk round the slipway on to the beach. Leave the beach by the gap in the cliff where a stream flows out into the sea.

Follow the path on the right which heads towards a corner of fencing on the lower right-hand skyline. This path gradually climbs beside the gorge which carries the stream. As you reach the corner of the fencing you are overlooking the Chapman's Pool car park; soon you reach an abandoned wartime building.

From here a track leads ahead to Hill Bottom where it joins the tarred road. Follow this up the hill, to the right, and pass through Renscombe Farm to return to Worth Matravers. ●

Below Renscombe

Photograph: Rodney Legg

Dancing Ledge and Priest's Way

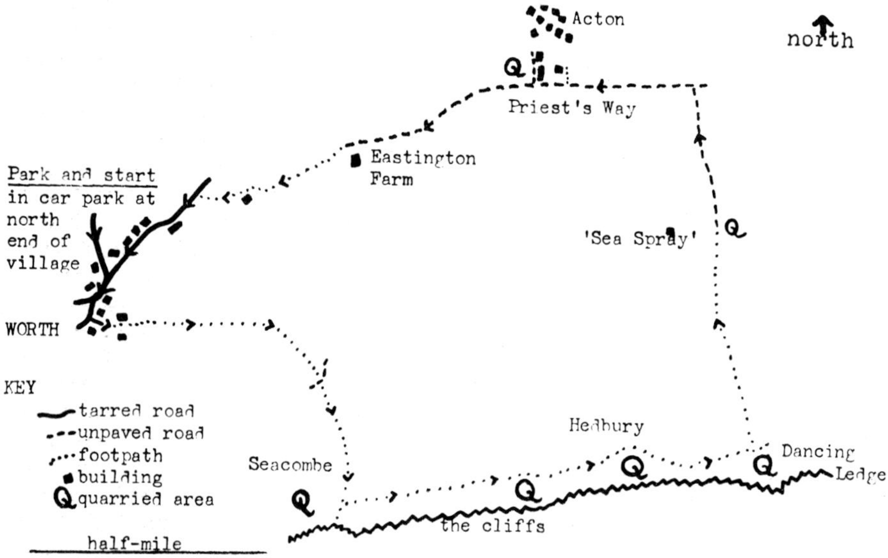

THE ALTERNATIVE walk from Worth Matravers is to head east instead of west. This also covers *five* miles. The earlier route included Winspit and Chapman's Pool. The first half-mile of both walks ar the same but this one then continues on to the rocky ledges at Seacombe, beneath Purbeck's most extensive cliff quarries. It then goes eastward to Dancing Ledge and the Priest's Way, the ancient trackway linking Worth and Swanage, its name a reminder of the time when each was small and joined ecclesiastically.

This is a walk where one of the field-guides on wild flowers would be useful. In all the fields above the sea — except those that have been "improved" by ploughing and then re-seeded to grass — the turf is dense with the full range of limestone flora, including prolific orchid colonies.

Park in Worth Matravers village car park. This is on the Kingston road, the road you enter the village on if you come from Corfe, a short distance north of the Square and Compasses public house. There is an honesty-box set in a stone.

Turn right on leaving the car park and walk down the slope to the road junction below the Square and Compasses. Turn right here and walk down to the village green. Turn left just before the duck pond and then continue to the left after you pass a house called "Lowgill". This short piece of road has a "no through road" symbol, and after that there is "bus stop" painted on the tarmac. Facing you is a signpost: "Footpath to Seacombe."

Walk around the bend, and the path is then signposted between two stone

walls. At the end of this narrow stretch the path emerges on to a field. Walk straight ahead across the field, descending the slope and then walk up the other side to the stone wall on the skyline. About 30 yards from this top right-hand corner of the field there is a low

Seacombe quarries

Courtesy: Mervyn E Jones

piece of wall with a sign "public footpath".

Cross the wall here and walk straight ahead, along the grass strip between two arable fields. You are soon overlooking Seacombe valley. At the end of the field there is a signpost "Footpath to Seacombe" pointing you downhill to the bottom right-hand corner of the field. In the field on your right there are some very clear mediaeval strip lynchet cultivation terraces. In the lower corner of the field there is a gate and another signpost to Seacombe. From here onwards, to the quarry at Hedbury, it is National Trust land.

Walk between some ivy-covered hawthorns and then follow the tall hedge which grows from the remains of an old stone wall, running towards the sea at the centre of the valley. At the end of the hedge the valley bends to the right and here you cross a stony track.

Follow the less clearly defined path, which continues down the middle of the valley, beside the bulrushes of a dried-up ditch and heading directly towards the sea. To the right the hillside has been heavily quarried.

At the end of the path you can walk down a gash in the cliff, across rocky ledges to the sea. On leaving the shore at Seacombe you turn east along the cliff in the direction of Swanage (a right turn if you have your back to the sea) and follow a sign saying "Coast path, Dancing Ledge 1". At the top of the slope, after the debris of a stone wall, there is a dome-shaped iron hood of a 1940 gun emplacement, overlooking the valley. Follow the cliff-top fence. You pass one small cliff-side quarry shelf, and then a far larger one. This second deserted quarry is Hedbury and on the main ledge above the sea there is a seven-foot Georgian cannon mounted on a modern stone plinth and facing out to sea.

Continue along the cliff to the next quarry shelf, which is at a lower level with ledges that are washed by the sea at high tide. Here, at Dancing Ledge, a milestone says "Coast path, Seacombe 1". From this point you go inland.

Turn left at this stone, and keep the stone wall on your right for about 40 yards. The path then veers slightly leftward, and you head for the dip in the horizon facing you.

There is a broken stone wall and a patch of scrub at the end of the field.

Cross the wall, over two fence bars, near the main patch of blackthorn scrub. Continue straight ahead and follow the path uphill along a gully. At the top end of the field there is a wire fence.

Go through the iron gate beside it, and then follow the cart track which continues straight ahead, beside a stone wall. There is an isolated house obscured by a wooded garden across the field to your left. Originally known as King's Ground Cottages, it is now called Sea Spray. At the top of the rise you pass a working stone quarry, and keep walking ahead. The track is now very firm and well-defined.

Turn left at its junction with another main track. Here there are two stones, one telling you that you have come from Dancing Ledge, and the other saying: "Priest's Way, Worth $1\frac{1}{2}$".

As you walk towards Worth you pass the quarrymen's hamlet of Acton, its surrounding land deeply gouged by opencast pits. When it passes Acton the Priest's Way continues straight ahead and it does not actually go through the hamlet.

The next habitation is in half-a-mile at Eastington, where a farmstead has numerous stone-walled sheds. After it has passed the entrance to the farm, the Priest's Way goes between two gate posts and is

Wartime machine gun post of the type that survives above Seacombe

Photograph: Imperial War Office

no longer bordered by stone walls. **Here you turn off the track, to the left, and follow the left-hand wall around the edge of the first field.** Then walk straight across the grass pasture to an electricity pole in the middle of the field. Keep walking ahead, at the top of the slope, to a gap with four iron bars in the wall facing you.

Follow the left-hand edge of this field, and around the pine trees by the garden of a house. Cross the concrete drive and then turn a little towards the right. Aim for the asbestos barn on the nearby skyline. To the right of it there is a stile on to the road.

Cross this and turn left along the road, walking into Worth Matravers. Turn right at the Square and Compasses public house and walk back to your car. ●

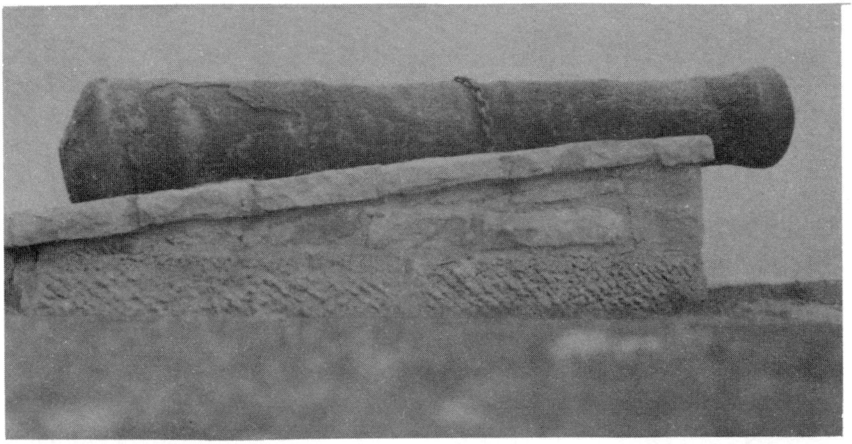

Cannon at Hedbury Quarry — Photograph: Rodney Legg

Dancing Ledge — Photograph: William Powell

Durlston Country Park

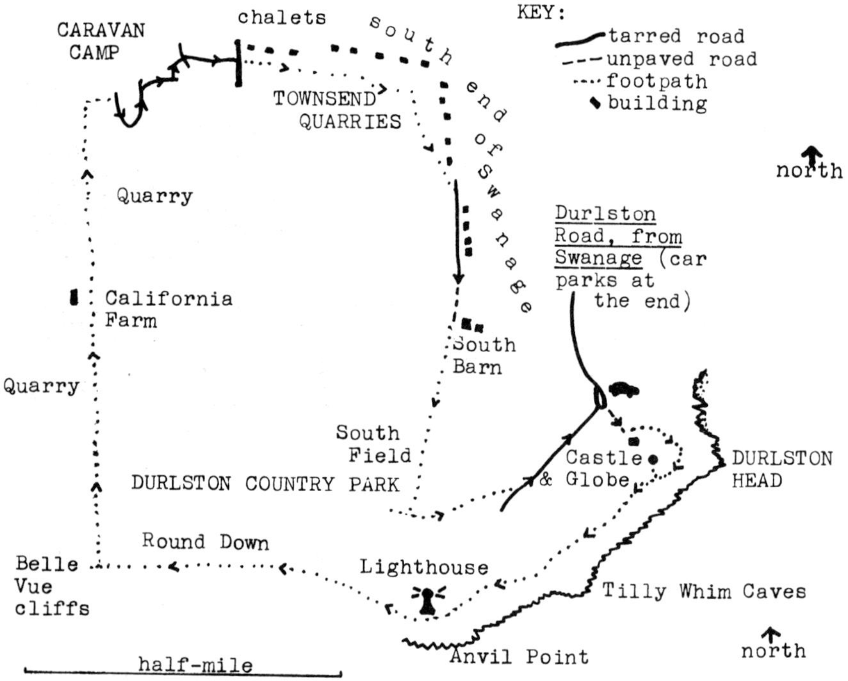

THE CLIFFS south of Swanage were chosen in the early 1970s for Dorset's first country park and a significant holding of council land, already highly popular with visitors, was expanded by leasing adjoining fields. This was a Victorian and Edwardian playground with plenty of the history of seaside tourism as well as important wildlife habitats. In 1974 Durlston Park was opened. County planning officer Alan Swindall explained that the management plan had been designed to preserve "the rich ecological pattern" by a "careful balance between people and nature". It includes some of the last sea-cliff nesting sites of the auks, and concentrations of orchids across Round Down.

The park incorporates Durlston Head and its Great Globe, Anvil Point and a subterranean access problem in the form of Tilly Whim Caves which were closed through fear of accidents. Inland, the park extends half a mile, to within one field of California Farm, Durlston Farm and South Barn. On the western edge it joins the National Trust's Belle Vue holding.

This *five* mile walk explores them all, and also brings in the superbly wild Dorset Naturalists' Trust reserve in the old Townsend Quarries above the south side of Swanage;

George Burt's stone Globe Courtesy: Dorset County Magazine

Cliff quarries at Tilly Whim Caves Courtesy: Dorset County Magazine

though to find a suitable linking path we have to take you through caravans. The wardening at Durlston is low-profile but demanding, with plenty of the problems happening at anti-social hours, and on this walk there is much greater scope than usual for roaming at will. Take great care if the seabirds lure you to the cliffs. There is one notice at Durlston which you are asked to observe as a matter of course on this and any other walk: "Please leave the flowers for everyone to enjoy."

If you come into Swanage along the main road from Corfe Castle, the A 351, you follow the "Durlston" signs which bring you into built-up Swanage through Kings Road West. You then pass the bus station and turn right at a mini roundabout, into the main shopping centre. Turn right at the end of this street, into the main road along the back of the seafront — along which anyone from the Studland side of Purbeck will be coming towards Durlston. You then briefly follow the sea and turn right just before the Pier Head Restaurant, steeply uphill beside the Peveril open space. Half-way up the hill you turn left into Durlston Road and follow it all the way, through Swanage suburbia, on to the downs. You pass "15" mph markers and are inside Durlston Country Park. At the end of the road there is a turning circle with car-parks on both sides.

Take the first, left-hand car park, if there are vacancies. The walk begins through its southern side, along a rough track with a notice: "Delivery vehicles only." It is signposted to the "Castle Cafe and Bar, Coast Path, Great Globe." You turn a corner to face the Durlston Head Castle, a large corbel-turreted restaurant set on the cliffs and surrounded by innumerable tablets of stone inscribed with statistics and poetry. It is a palatial French riviera-style villa of Purbeck stone, on land George Burt had bought in 1864. Three granite pillars were ordered by Sir Charles Barry for Trafalgar Square but turned out to be surplus and were inscribed by Burt: "Durlston Head Castle, above sea 215 feet."

Take the second track downhill on the left, beside the castle wall. Keep turning right, to make a circuit of the headland. From it you look north into Durlston and Swanage Bays. The first bay has tumbled cliffs where the remains of some of the first marsupials have been found, from the beginning of the age of mammals. Old Harry Rocks are visible in the distance, and Bournemouth seafront beyond. Out to sea, on a clear day, is the tip of the Isle of Wight, at the Needles. At the end of the headland is another of Burt's information stones: "Above sea 111 ft." Just around the corner you come to a flight of steps to the Great Globe. It weighs forty tons, is ten feet in diameter, and is carved in Portland stone, showing continents, oceans and rivers. It was made in sections at Mowlem's Greenwich works in 1887, and brought to Swanage in fifteen segments. It is "Above sea 136 ft." The information tablets behind it are dated 1891. At the same scale, we are told, "The Sun would be 1090 ft 0 ins" and "The Moon 2 feet 9 ins." The fastest object in our skies is named: "The common black swift flies at the rate of 200 miles per hour." On the other hand: "The Sun rotates once in 25 days: so a point on the solar equator is whirled round with a velocity of 4,500 miles an hour." "The distance from the Earth to the nearest fixed Star Alpha Centauri, visible in the southern hemisphere, is computed to be 200,000 times that of the Sun. Light which travels at the rate of about 186,000 miles a second would be three and a half years in reaching the Earth from this Star." Enough, says Blaise Pascal: "Our nature consists in motion: perfect rest is death." Notice to the left of the exit a large scratched stone carved at the top: "Persons wishing to write their names will please do so on this stone only." Some have taken up the offer, and the tablets are not sub-

The view from Durlston Head, across Peveril Point to Ballard Down

Photograph: William Powell

jected to graffiti.

Walk back down the steps on to the coastal path and turn right along it. A modern notice board gives you drawings of the "Birds of the sea-cliffs" and tells you to expect fulmars, kittiwakes, razorbills, guillemots, shags and herring gulls – which you will already have heard. The path westward has its own poetry: "An iron coast and angry waves/You seem to hear them rise and fall/And roar rock – thwarted in their bellowing caves/Beneath the windy wall. Above the sea 149 ft."

You are approaching Anvil Point lighthouse. Before you reach it you pass the entrance to Tilly Whim Caves, which were closed at the time of writing because of rock-falls. Notice, however, the "1887" stone to the left of the entrance. These three octagonal pieces of granite stood beside Pentonville prison and were brought here when George Burt had this entrance into the old quarries blown out to provide a direct access into the caverns that avoided people having to stray on to another owner's land. Inside he added an inscription to the wall of the first gallery with a potted history: "These caves were formed centuries ago by men making sinks and rick-stones. Smuggling was also carried out here, and both were discontinued about the end of the French Wars, 1814." You next pass a steel tower with a triangle on top; the eastern of two sea-marks for a measured nautical mile, used in sea trials. From the lighthouse side of the valley you can look back into the two surviving openings of Tilly Whim and the collapsed end one. Tilly was a person and the "whim" a crane used to lower stones onto boats.

Walk on the sea-side of the lighthouse. There is a modern notice to add to the Durlston collection. "The public are advised that a fog signal emitting a very loud noise may be sounded in this vicinity at any time without prior warning."

From the lighthouse you turn fractionally inland, and climb to the top of the hill overlooking the coast. This is the hill immediately to the right of the cliffs. It is Round Down, though not so smooth now as it is heavily cratered by quarrying. At the centre are the foundations of a naval signal station of the Napoleonic period. It would have had a huge semaphore with shuttering in the shapes of squares and circles. At the end of the Round Down you cross a stone stile into the National Trust's Belle Vue cliffs.

Then turn right, to head inland, and keep the stone wall on your right. You pass an active set of quarries, with stone ranging in size from great boulders down to the occasional piles of neatly-shaped blocks. Follow the footpath signs and walk at the bottom of the garden at California Farm. The farmer has a view down the valley to the Isle of Wight, which takes in the entire western coast to St. Catherine's Point. On a clear morning he can lie in bed and tell the direction of the wind from the flares at Fawley oil refinery. Burt would be interested to know that the flares in the Gulf are the first man-made sight that this planet offers to astronauts returning from the moon – waste is something we do so well.

You descend into a caravan camp. On crossing its boundary you turn immediately right, through a gap in the hedge, and then turn right again along the tarred road.

Follow the drive as it swings leftward, downhill, to pass the lavatory block. Turn right opposite caravan plot 39, and walk uphill passing numbers 54, 53 and 43A. Turn left opposite No. 47, downhill. You now have a view over Swanage and across to Ballard Down.

Turn right at the crossroads between caravan plots 132 and 185. You then fork right, passing "car space 184", and caravans 173, 174, 178 and 179.

Cross over the tarred road, half way up a hill, and follow the yellow "Footpath" marker on the other side. This corner of the 19th century Townsend Quarries does not have caravans, and is a nature reserve managed by Dorset Naturalists' Trust. Between the spoil heaps you pass an underground shaft, a grilled gap at the top of which provides a crucial refuge for bats of up to 17 species. The remains of stones a few yards from the entrance are its crabstones. These held a capstan, which was powered by a donkey on a circular path, to haul carts of stone from a hundred feet underground. There are a maze of paths between the thickets.

The point you aim for is at the right-hand southern -upper- **end of Swanage where the conifers start to outnumber the houses.** The group of houses next to this part of the quarries have dormer windows.

Here you come on to a tarred road and turn right along it, uphill. From the top of the ridge it becomes a stony track, straight ahead to a farmstead. Continue straight ahead from the South Barn, uphill through rough pastureland. After the next stone wall you are back inside Durlston Country Park. This flat expanse was South Field, one of the three main areas of cultivation strips for mediaeval Swanage. Continue straight ahead, keeping the stone walls to your left. You come to a gate at the head of the valley overlooking the lighthouse.

Turn left here, along the main grassy path to the lighthouse road. Turn left along the road, and follow it back to the car-parks. ●

Anvil Point lighthouse Photograph: Colin Graham

Old Harry and Ballard Down

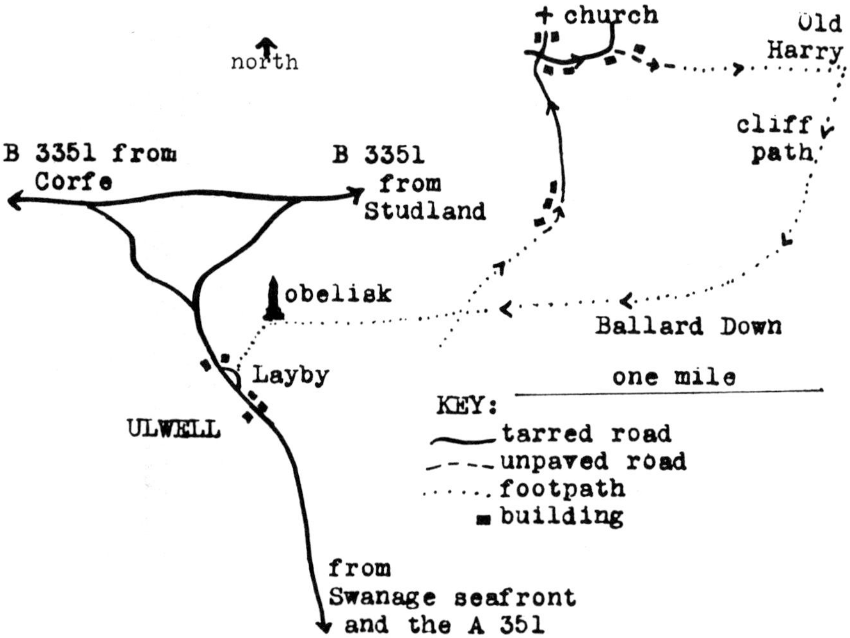

THIS IS the ideal Purbeck coastal walk for hot summer afternoons. The tracks are all clearly marked, without a single obstruction, and the only tough section is a steepish climb at the beginning. Its length is *five miles* and the walk has views all the way. All of the route is on National Trust land, being included within the great bequest of Ralph Bankes who died on 19 August 1981.

Another advantage is that it starts from what is usually the only empty layby in an otherwise traffic-clogged Isle of Purbeck. The layby is at Ulwell beside the link road that runs through the Purbeck Hills from Swanage to Studland and connects the B 3351 with the A 351. Its location is easy to pinpoint as there happens to be a "Welcome to Swanage" mural in tiles by the roadside. If you want to find the position on the Ordnance Survey map, the grid reference is 022809.

Park and start in the main roadside layby at Ulwell beside the "Welcome to Swanage" stone. In the hedgerow facing this sign there is a wicket gate and the notice: "S.U.D.C. Public footpath leading to Studland."

Go through this and walk uphill along a well-marked track. Beside the path is a granite boundary stone engraved: "Swanage 1883." The track leads to the right and climbs the hillside, following a wire fence beside some gorse bushes.

At the top is a 20-foot obelisk (rebuilt 1973) set into the side of a Bronze Age burial mound. Say the tablets at the base: "This obelisk was placed here by George Burt to commemorate the introduction of pure water from the chalk formation to Swanage. The granite was taken down from near the Mansion House, London, and erected here in 1892." Yet another stone proclaims: "Swanage Water Act 1883. 489 feet above sea level." What none of the stonework tells you is that this obelisk, when in London, was a lamp standard.

Turn right at the obelisk, along the hilltop track, and past another "Swanage 1883" stone. Keep walking straight ahead when you pass a "Footpath to Studland" sign. About 500 yards after this post you reach a hilltop crossroads where a path comes up the slope from Swanage.

Turn left, over a stile, and walk downhill towards Studland. You pass a stone seat with the wording: "Rest and be thankful."

Turn right where you emerge on a chalky road in a cluster of modern houses. This becomes a tarred road and brings you to the stump of the village cross (a lump of heathstone five feet across) at the centre of Studland.

Turn right, downhill, along the road signposted to "The Beach." If, however, you have the time it is worth walking straight ahead for a few yards to see Studland's Saxon church which is not only among the oldest but also one of the most beautiful in Dorset.

The road to the beach runs through a deep elm-shrouded hollow and then bends to the left. Here you leave the road and carry on straight ahead along a track signposted "Bridleway and footpath to Swanage via Old Harry," beside a white-washed thatched cottage where they sell dressed crabs.

Keep walking ahead where the track is joined by another outside

Ulwell's gas-lamp obelisk

Photograph: John Pitfield

Old Harry Rocks Photograph: Roland Tarr

the village. Walk to Old Harry and then continue along the top of the towering white cliffs towards Swanage. Apart from Old Harry, there are another two jagged teeth of chalk standing offshore, known as the Pinnacles. Underneath is a sea-cave named Parson's Barn and so-called because nothing was larger or more accommodating in the days of the tithe!

When Swanage Bay comes into view the fence swings to the right and you climb Ballard Down. At the top is a concrete Ordnance Survey triangulation pillar. Follow the chalky path beside this, through a dyked earthwork, and then walk straight ahead along the top of the ridge.

This path runs in a straight line for well over a mile and brings you back to the obelisk. Here you turn left, over the stile, and descend to the road and your car. ●

Photograph: Frederick G Masters

The Pinnacles off Ballard Down

Courtesy: National Trust

Nine Barrow Down and Rempstone

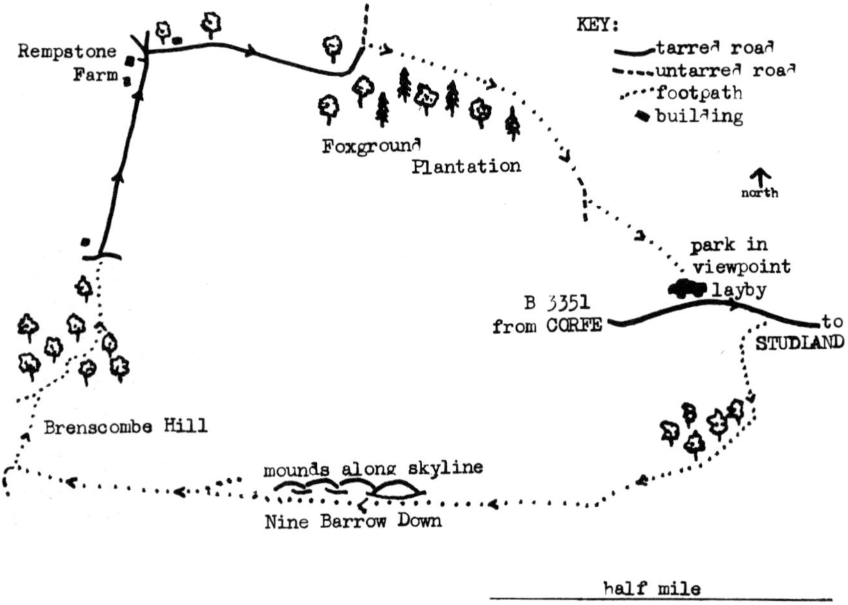

THIS SHORT walk of *four* miles is another based upon the convenient viewpoint layby above Studland Heath, beside the B3351 on the Corfe side of the Purbeck golf course. It heads in a different direction from previous walks, to the summit of the Purbeck Hills, and along Nine Barrow Down which as you might have guessed is amongst the treasures which passed into National Trust ownership in 1982. Then for variety there is woodland and the fringes of the heath at Rempstone. It is all easy walking country with tracks that are clearly defined though there may be some mud on the heathland parts after wet weather.

As you approach Corfe Castle along the main road from Wareham, the A351, you turn off opposite the Castle hill. This is the B3351 and it is signposted "Studland 5". The road goes under a railway bridge and you continue for just over three miles. At the brow of a hill there is a 'P' sign off the left hand side of the road. There is parking at this viewpoint layby for about 20 to 25 cars, and a West Country Tourist Board information display which has been usefully redesigned to tell you about the heath below — since our complaints that the previous version was mainly about the Newfoundland fisheries!

Walk along the road in the Studland direction. There is a path along the top of the bank on the left-hand side, which keeps you above the threat of the traffic.

About 30 yards after the brow of the hill you turn right, through a black painted pair of gates. One is double sized and the other single, with a bridleway sign on it. A sunken trackway bends uphill. It brings you to another pair of gates, and there is then a raised section of trackway across open ground followed by another sunken way that leads to a wood on the side of the Purbeck Hills. This is National Trust land.

The ancient trackway passes an old chalkpit and climbs to the summit of the hill on Kingswood Down. As you leave the ash wood, continue straight ahead, gradually climbing to the top of the hill.

A fence-line, with clumps of gorse, runs along the ridge of the hill. In a short distance you come to an iron gate (with a "Please keep the gate shut" notice) and cross into the next field. Continue as before, now keeping the fence to your right. You are overlooking the Swanage valley. At the end of the field, a little to the left of the corner, is a wooden gate ("Keep shut") into the next stretch of downland.

The land to the left of the track is gorse covered. This block of unimproved chalkland passed into National Trust ownership with the rest of the Bankes estate in 1982, and contains the most important group of prehistoric burial mounds in Purbeck. In a quarter of a mile you pass a Neolithic long barrow and the line of Bronze Age burial mounds that straddle Nine Barrow Down. These were part of Ralph Bankes's estate and are now in National Trust ownership.

Corfe Castle comes into view in the dip in the hills and you join a well-worn chalky track. This heads directly towards the castle, on to a lower section of downland. At the foot of the slope there is a gate and stile and a level section of track that continues on the top of the ridge for a third of a mile.

It then bends sharply downhill to the left but here you turn right, keeping the hedge to your right, and

Viewpoint layby on the road between Corfe Castle and Studland Photograph: Rodney Legg

head towards Hamworthy power station and Brownsea Island. The path passes through scrub and enters oak and hazel woodland.

You join a sunken chalky trackway that runs through the wood to the tarred road. Cross over, into the lane marked "Rempstone ½". On your left, beside the drive to Bushey House, is a phoney 1970s stone circle, of 19 sandstone boulders which might look a little more convincing without the suburban weeping willow planted at the centre. At Rempstone you pass a cottage, house and farm, at the four-way road junction beside the barns.

Here you turn right. Then you pass a "Beware Adders" sign and a wooden ex-Methodist church now labelled "Rempstone H & D C.Y.C." which has something to with canoes. The lane continues past a barn and into the trees, where Rempstone adders foresake their natural open habitats for dank woodland. Perhaps Darwin was wrong and evolution does move through sudden jumps.

At the end of the wood there is a sign "Foxground, bridleway only" and immediately after this you turn right through a wooden gate. A public footpath follows the edge of the wood. At the end of the field there is a stile and you continue straight ahead on the other side, up the slope. At the top there is a break in the fence into a cleared field.

Continue to keep the wood to your right. You then come into open ground and follow the fence, continuing straight ahead towards the hills. You are now moving in a direct line towards your car in the layby. At the end of the field there is an iron gate.

On the other side you walk straight across the middle of the field, using a public footpath that runs up to the left-hand end of the layby. There is a stile in the fence, near the corner, and another into the left-hand end of the layby. ●

The genuine Rempstone stone circle, before it became hidden in a dense plantation. It lies on the south side of the main road, just under a mile from the viewpoint layby in the Corfe direction

Photograph: Rodney Legg

Purbeck Forest and the Agglestone

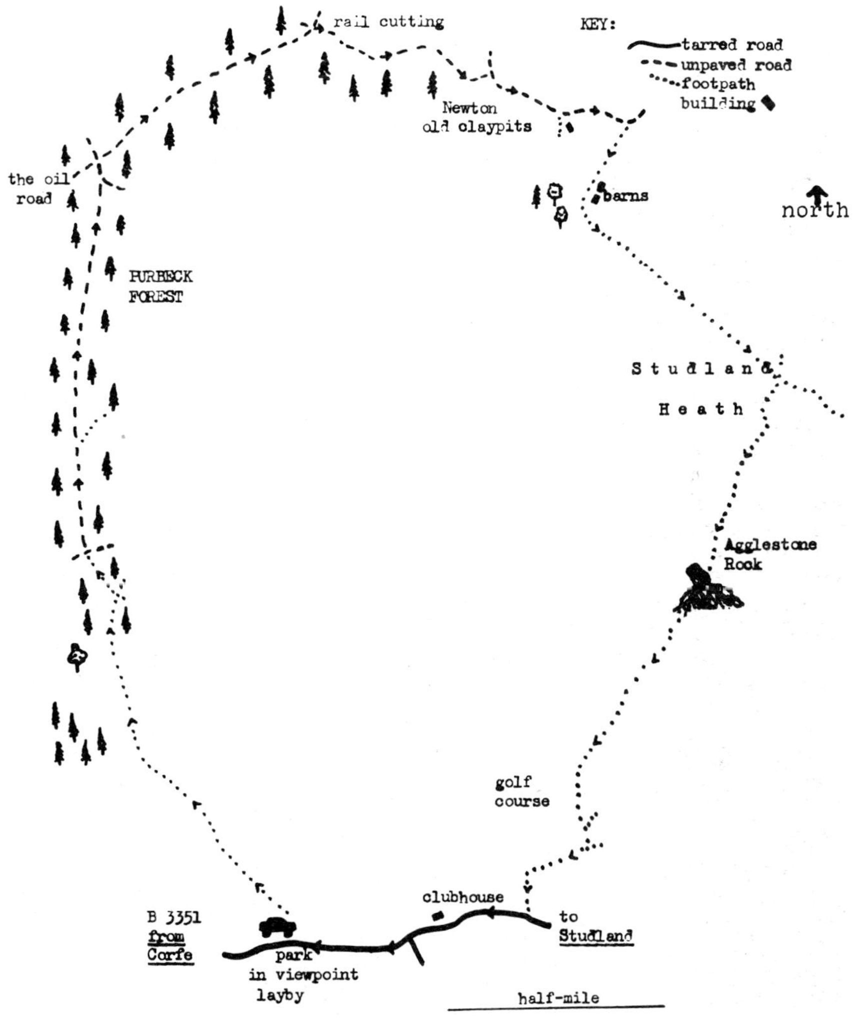

THERE ARE no longer many corners of Dorset where you can embark on a *seven* mile walk across unspoilt heathland. Or, at least, an enclave of a fast receding landscape where the intrusions are just about palatable — in this case being two miles of plantation pines (some hiding oil wells), a few pastures claimed from the heather, and a scenically-sited golf course. This walk is into the backlands of

Studland in Purbeck, with Poole Harbour for the wallpaper on one side and the range of hills on the other. Changes make for constant variety, in an area where before 1947 you would have experienced total ecological sameness, with moors on the scale of a mini-Yorkshire. The paths across it are dry and well worn. They bring you out of the wilderness and up to the great Agglestone rock, thrown by the devil from the Isle of Wight (aiming at Corfe Castle). It was a lousy shot, but he was probably drunk at the time. The natural history chances in this area are higher than average, with such delights in late summer as tiny blue gentians beside the bogs, three foot anthills in the pines, and plenty of dragonflies. There are sika deer, red deer of Japan, in the woods. Winter brings flocks of geese to the southern inlets of Poole Harbour, and birds of prey slip across the heath.

As you approach Corfe Castle along the main road from Wareham, the A351, you turn off opposite the Castle hill. This is the B3351 and it is signposted "Studland 5". The road goes under a railway bridge and you continue for just over three miles.

At the brow of a hill there is a 'P' sign off the left hand side of the road. There is parking at this view-point layby for about 20 to 25 cars, and a West Country Tourist Board information display telling you about Poole Harbour.

Walk to the far end of the layby, in the Studland direction, and then go downhill from the rubbish container, over a stile into the field. Go over to the next stile in the fence facing you, about 50 yards from the corner. You are now heading for the left-hand extremity of Poole Harbour, in the middle distance.

Cross the next field diagonally, to the iron gate in the opposite corner. A dirt track leads into the following field and takes you towards the right-hand corner of the nearest block of woodland, by the electricity poles. About a hundred yards before the corner of the wood the track bends away from the fence and heads slightly right of centre. You come to the corner of another field and follow this fence straight ahead, downhill towards the extreme left-hand end of the harbour. There is the remains of an old trackway, littered with fragments of heathstone. Follow this fence for its entirety, beside an area of heathland, to a gate into the Forestry Commission plantation.

The track continues into the wood, crossing a brackish stream and going uphill to join a gravel ride. Continue straight ahead, up the slope between the 30-year-old stands of pine.

After about a hundred yards you turn off the main track, and go into the trees. There is a faint blue arrow on one of the trunks. This narrow grassy ride comes out at a T-junction of gravel tracks.

Continue straight across, taking the widest of the options. Keep on this main track for a mile, ignoring — a third of a mile along — a blue bridleway arrow that points to another right-of-way. You come in a mile to another track, joining from the right, which you also ignore. Then there is a crossroads, beneath a power line.

Turn right along the road, which was constructed in 1905 as a mineral railway, with steam engines carrying clay across the heath from Norden near Corfe to a wharf at Goathorn. It was abandoned in 1937, and now carries oil exploration traffic.

In half a mile the road bends to the right, and to your left for some distance you can see a section of the original railway cutting. Goathorn Farm then comes into view and the bridleway forks right, away from the main track. This area is known as Newton, from Edward I's failed

Smooth snake — Britain's rarest reptile and the main reason for the creation of Studland Heath national nature reserve. It is harmless to us

Photographs: Nature Conservancy

Sand lizard — the smooth snake's principal prey

scheme to establish a new town here, as an export centre for the marble trade. You then come to another track and the bridleway turns to the right, across a concrete bridge. A few yards away, to the left, are the heathstone foundations of a house about 30 feet long by 15 feet wide, with the remains of one last collapsed window. This is all that has survived, from any period, of Newton. The track is then sandy, and to your left you can see Brand's Bay, which is blue or brown depending on the tide. In about 200 yards, to your right behind the gorse bushes, is an old claypit filled with water, which refracts blueish-green light. The bottom is white, with lumps of ball clay.

The track then bends to the left, at a clearing beside Greenland Cottage, and goes through a gate, to pass between mixed hedgerows that have plenty of holly. A concrete bridge crosses a brackish stream. Look out for sika deer slots in the unlikely location of the middle of the mud in the next piece of brown water.

At the top of the rise you turn right, along a track that has a notice about keeping dogs on leads when using rights-of-way through the farm. The path follows a fence to a gate: "Please close my gate. My husband's 'Fresian' and there are draughts around my calves. Moo. Hope you enjoy your walk." You pass two barns (and no sign of the husband). The track then goes through two iron gates. After the second the path, which is now grassy, bends to the left. There is another gate with a notice, asking you to keep the gate closed to avoid loss of cattle.

In this field there are two rights-of-way and the one you want goes to the left, diagonally across the centre, to a wooden hunting gate about 50 yards to the right of the far corner. Continue across the corner of the next field to an iron gate on to Studland Heath. Go a little to the left, but only a few feet, and then on the right you'll see a trackway uphill into the gorse. The track then crosses the heather, and you aim for a point a little to the left of the belt of woodland on the horizon. All of

Agglestone — 400 tons of rock said to have been thrown by the Devil, from the Isle of Wight, at Corfe Castle (it missed)
Photograph: John Pitfield

the rest of the walk is owned by the National Trust, having been acquired in the Bankes bequest of 1982.

The next gate is marked "Keep this gate closed to prevent loss of cattle." You are now on the Nature Conservancy Council's Studland national nature reserve. Damp ruts are enlivened by insect-eating sundews, and tussocks of white cotton grass. After about half a mile you go straight over at a crossing of tracks. In a quarter of a mile the track then descends towards an area of birch scrub.

Just before the first trees you turn right, along a sandy path that heads directly towards the Agglestone rock, silhouetted on the skyline. Walk up to the Agglestone. This great mass of iron impregnated sandstone has protected the rest of the hill from erosion, but collapsed on to its side ten years ago. It is surrounded by a sandy dustbowl.

From here the path winds uphill for about half a mile and skirts the edge of the Isle of Purbeck Golf Course. Fork right when the path gives you two choices, and keep the golf links in view. You finally come out facing one of the greens, with an open view into the Frome valley beyond.

Turn left, along a path between the fence and a hedge. Go through a wooden gate on to a layby and the tarred road.

Turn right along the road and walk back to your car, which is half a mile away. Take care to walk towards the oncoming traffic. For most of the way, however, there is a footpath along the bank above the road. Ignore the turn-off to Swanage, and climb on to the verge to avoid any encounters with cars at the next corner. Your car is just over the next brow. ●

A glance back across Studland Heath to the Agglestone Photograph: Frederick G Masters

Ower and Poole Harbour

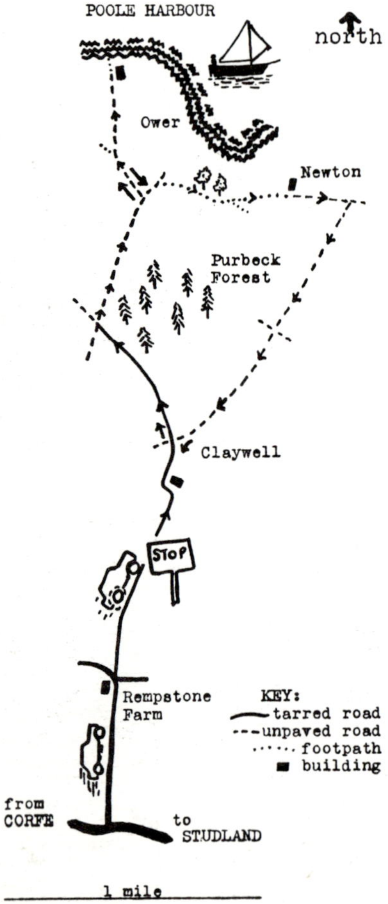

OF ALL OUR Purbeck walks, this is the simplest. It is a walk of only *four* miles across dry, sandy heathland to the southern shore of Poole Harbour. There is only one stile to climb and just two gates that have to be opened. There are no hills to climb and only a few very gentle slopes that rise to barely 75 feet above the harbour water level. This is a walk for any time of the year and its clearly defined tracks run through the Forestry Commission's Purbeck Forest and emerge on remnants of the Great Heath. Drive to Corfe Castle and take the B3551 road (under the railway bridge) which goes to Studland.

Note the left turns off this road. Firstly, "Wytch 2". Secondly, "Bushey". **Thirdly, "Rempstone Farm". Take this third one: it is on the brow of a hill two miles out from Corfe and beside a clump of old pine trees.**

This road opens out with wide grass verges at the farm. It bends to the left after the buildings but you go straight ahead (at the No Through Road sign) on this corner.

Park at the "Rempstone Estates, No Motors" sign where this road passes between two white gate posts. Walk along this tarred road for as far as it goes. It is a sheltered track between stands of Scots pine. At the end of the tarred surface the road forks on to two stony tracks.

Take the right fork with the arrowed sign "Water 660 yards." This leads to Ower Farm. The track crosses a brackish stream at a cattlegrid and then climbs a short slope.

Turn left at the top along a track which joins at a 'T' junction.

Fork right through an iron gate which is normally open. Follow this track to the isolated building in the middle of the long, low horizon. This is Ower Passage and a notice says: "Please walk through and close gate." Continue straight

High water at Ower Passage — Photograph: Rodney Legg

Nineteenth century duck-punts on Poole Harbour — Courtesy: Dorset County Magazine

ahead, alongside a cottage, to the beach. All of the Purbeck marble that went to great churches all across England was shipped out from this very point. Ower Passage was the port for the most important of Dorset's mediaeval industries. But there is another attraction as, at high tide, this place can claim to be one of the most beautiful in Dorset. It is certainly the most peaceful. The impressive heather-clad slopes rising from the harbour, to the right, are Green Island. Enjoy this spot as Ower Passage is what the walk is for and, when you have had enough, turn back the way you came.

This time, turn left when you arrive back at the "Ower Farm and Cottage" notice at the 'T' junction. Make sure you only follow this track for a few yards, to the top of the slope, and go through an iron gate on the right by the second telegraph pole. This path passes a holly wood, Game Copse, and then follows a rise above Newton Bay which in winter is one of the finest, and certainly the loneliest, part of Poole Harbour for watching wildfowl.

Leave the track and go straight towards the white-painted house. Immediately to the right of this house there is a stile. Climb over and continue ahead. This public path climbs on to the heath and passes a "Dedicated Tree Area, Private" sign. Stop shortly after this (as you go under a power line by a black iron gate) where a track joins you from the right.

Turn abruptly right to take this track which has a sign "Forestry Commission, Purbeck." This road follows the course of the longest mineral railway line in Dorset which carried clay to Poole Harbour until the outbreak of the last war. Continue straight ahead at the first woodland crossroads but stop at the second crossroads where there is another "Forestry Commission, Purbeck" sign. Turn left along the tarred road and walk back to your car. ●

Approaching Ower Passage Photograph: Rodney Legg

PURBECK WALKS 19

Little Sea and Studland church

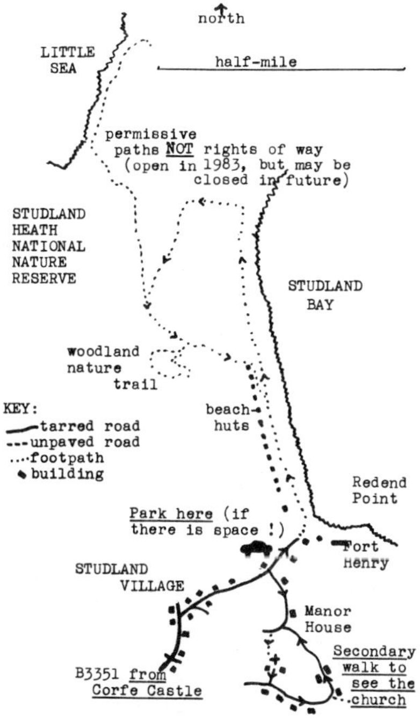

LEAVING THE summertime hordes at Studland beach you can wander inland to a remarkable variety of wildlife habitats. The vegetation is sufficiently hostile to prevent too much human penetration. The area abounds with wildlife, much of which no longer regards the human activity as posing much of a threat. These *four* miles of wanderings take in the few paths that skirt this fascinating seaside heathland. Most of the paths are into the Nature Conservancy's national nature reserve, which was extended to 1,500 acres in the 1970s, and the whole of the area came into National Trust ownership in 1982 as a result of Ralph Bankes's bequest. Despite this the general access to the Studland interior has to be minimised as much as possible and it is not the Conservancy or Trust policy to cut paths. The one or two that we use here do exist on the ground and have been walked in the past without challenge but as I shall remind you in the main text they are permissive rather than statutory and the position may change in the future.

There is an additional diversion at the end to see Studland church, which is one of the finest in Dorset, and into some rural corners of great charm. Be warned that in high summer the police sometimes close the B 3351 Studland road at Corfe Castle because of congestion, when the beach car-parks are completely full. Think of an alternative before you set out.

Drive into the centre of Studland village. Follow the signs to "Middle Beach car park" and then walk down Beach Road to the steps on to the sands. Visible to the right from the steps on to Studland beach are the sycamore-covered cliffs of Redend Point. You will spot a pillbox and a gun emplacement but end-on at the top, to the left of the pine trees, is the great Fort Henry observation post. This was used by Winston Churchill, Bernard Montgomery and Dwight D. Eisenhower for watching the practice invasion landings of 1943-44. It is off the public path network, but it is a major piece of our comparatively recent past. The walls are about three feet thick and there is an eye-level observation slit, recessed on the outside, running along just about its full ninety feet length. It is indestructible, until such time as the sea undermines these cliffs, and looks set to survive long enough to become an acknowledged treasure of the National Trust.

The "Coastal Path" is signposted northwards along the beach, to Shell Bay. The easiest walking is at the tide line, where the sand is damp and firm. Across the water, from right to left, you see Old Harry Rocks, the Needles on the Isle of Wight, and the cliffs from Barton-on-Sea, through Bournemouth, to Canford Cliffs. The shallows off Studland are known as the Milkmaid Bank. About a third of a mile after the lines of beach-huts there is a yellow marker post at the top of the beach.

Turn off here into a track through the sand dunes. It is a nature trail with a series of numbers on yellow concrete posts. The first three show the sands in a transitional state between early marram grass colonisation and the secondary growths of heather. This part is recent, having been consolidated over the past century or so. Then at bollard 4 you turn left to skirt an area of sallow and birch bog.

Turn right after bollard 5 and climb to the top of a more mature dune. From here you have a view inland to the Little Sea, which is now a freshwater lagoon. In the 1840s it was still open to the sea at the far right. Look out for pygmy and common shrews and harvest mice, as well as sand lizards and smooth snakes. Watch the skies for cormorants, curlew, the oyster-catchers and the occasional heron. At intermediate levels there are green woodpeckers, warblers, stonechats and wrens – and on the day I did the walk there was a large flock of long-tailed tits.

The track brings you towards the back parts of Studland beach. Look out for another track that gradually converges from the right.

Turn right along this track and pass a stand of fire-beaters. These are a reminder that this area is always a "High Fire Risk"; not that conservationists smoke. The track is a permissive path rather than a right of way, so please do not continue if at

Redend Point (right) with Old Harry Rocks in the background Photograph: E V Tanner

some later date it is blocked by signs. At the time of writing you can use a track through the heather as far as the Little Sea. The notice points out that there is "No boating or bathing".
Turn right to continue following the path, about twenty feet from the shore. The track extends half-way along the side of Little Sea and then peters out. You take your chances as to what you are going to see, but I disturbed a moorhen and then came face to face with a sandy-coloured fox whose chest was much whiter than usual.
Turn back along the track and return to Studland. There is a nature trail on your right just as a pillbox comes into view. This little circuit is through full woodland, with crows overhead, and is the final example of the wide variety of habitats in only a short distance. From here you must return to the human habitat, either by crossing the car-parks or returning to the beach.
Your car-park is off the Beach Road, which is up the steps after the Beach Office. If you still have some time, walk on to the first junction and turn left to pass the Manor House Hotel. Turn right at the next junction and then left after 25 yards. This footpath brings you to the cemetery and Studland church. Its walls are mainly of gritty local heathstone of warm reddish-brown tones. Roman burials have been found beside it. The present church is a mid-12th century elaboration of a simple late-Saxon church. The Royal Commission on Historical Monuments comments: "The building has a solid robustness of character which is impressive."
Continue out the main church gate, into the lane. On a mound at the end is the only mediaeval cross that has survived in Purbeck. The genuine part is the base, which is a circular block of heathstone four feet in diameter. The modern stone shaft was reconstructed in the 1970s. Stocks stood nearby until about 1850.
Turn left at the corner and then follow the road around to the left to bring you back to the junction by the Manor House Hotel. Turn right here and walk back to the junction near your car-park. This is to the right, unless, that is, the overcrowding forced you to abandon it elsewhere. ●

The robust lines of Studland church Photograph: Colin Graham

Shell Bay and Redhorn Quay

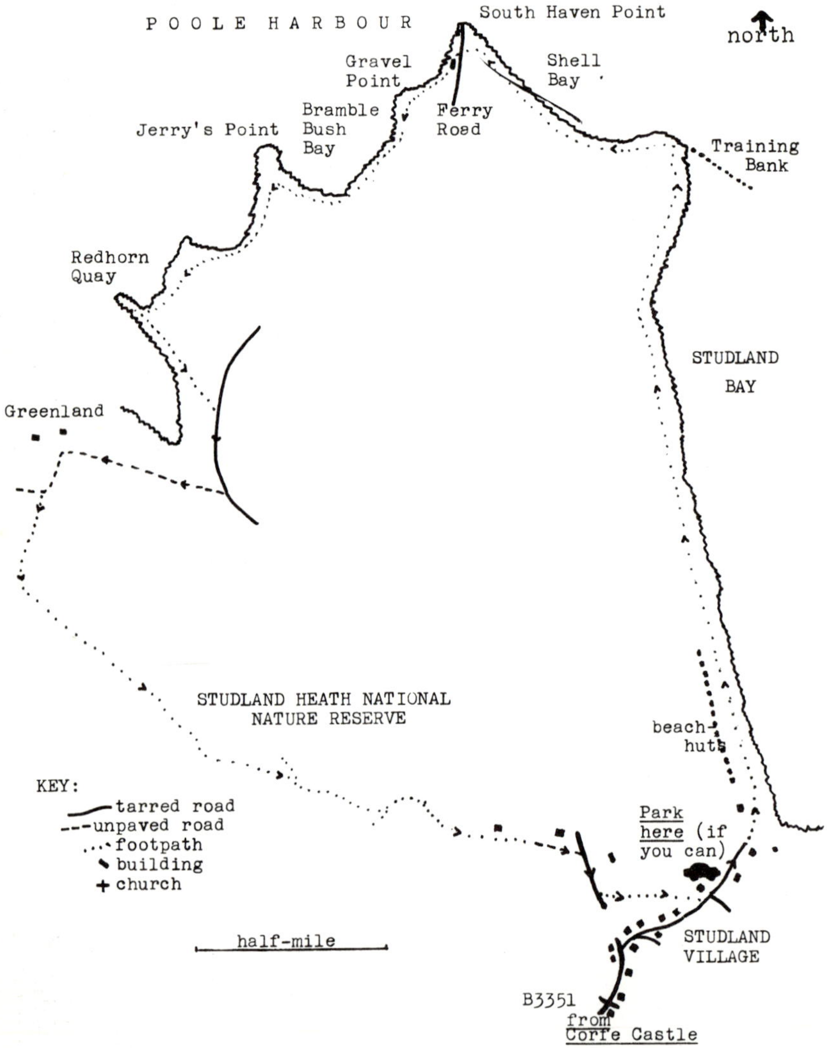

THE LONGER Studland Walk is offered with reservations. It is *seven* miles, most of which is sand and sky. This is a foreshore trek around Purbeck's north-eastern peninsula. It is a walk of considerable beauty but not universal appeal. As with our last walk it starts from Studland, which is liable to be sealed off on the best weekends in summer once the beach car-parks are full. The entire walk is on National Trust land.

Drive into the centre of Studland village. Follow the signs to "Middle

Beach car park" and then walk down Beach Road to the steps to the sands. Turn left along the "Coastal Path", northwards along the beach. The first couple of miles is the featureless bit, just endless sands and a steadily diminishing population as you approach the skyline. Listen for the singing sands, a distinct musical note being made as you tread the intermediate zone of about twelve yards between the high water mark and the start of the blown sands. But it is an elusive phenomenon. The first major man-made feature is the Training Bank which can be seen at low water jutting out for half a mile at the north end of Studland Bay. On this side of it are the shallow sands of the Milkmaid Bank, and on the other the Swash Channel shipping lane into Poole Harbour. With a bit of luck you'll be able to look up as something of considerable size, probably a cross-channel container vessel, enters or leaves the harbour. The Training Bank was constructed in the 1930s, its stone being brought from Corfe along the clay-railway across the heaths, as far as Goathorn Pier, and then shipped into place.

On turning the corner you are in Shell Bay — long regarded as Bournemouth's best beach, by adoption and tidal drift — and the view is across to the prosperous dwellings of Sandbanks peninsula. You turn the next corner, into Poole Harbour, at the slip-way of the chain ferry. You'll notice its chains dragging into the water. This is the South Haven Point, where an inn might nowadays do good business but it was allowed to collapse into the sands before the First World

Gravel Point to the South Haven Point, with Sandbanks across the water

Photograph: E Dodshon

Brownsea's south-eastern shore, from South Haven peninsula Photograph: E Dodshon

War. After the present buildings you come to Gravel Point which is all it claims. The view now is to Brownsea Castle and the island's southern cliffs. At low tide you lose these little bays completely and they become flat expanses of mud. But they do have the virtue of attracting the wading birds. The inlet after Gravel Point is known as Bramble Bush Bay and it brings you to Jerry's Point. This projects further across the mud and almost makes it to the deep-water channel of Stone Island Lake.

At the end of two more small bays, in almost a mile if you allow for the

Harbour foreshore and Brownsea Island Photograph: E. Dodshon

impossibility of walking a straight course, you come to Redhorn Quay. This projection must be walked to the tip. As its name suggests it was more than just a point in the middle of nowhere, being used to ship Purbeck stone and for the embarkation of the ferry route from Swanage and Studland to Poole. It still touches the deep-water channel at Redhorn Lake. Don't be deceived by the stones – blocks of granite were carried as ballast and have been dumped here. You are now looking across to the pine plantations on the Goathorn peninsula.

From here the shore is more marshy and you will have to divert inland, as far as the ferry road if necessary. Then **turn right,** along the track to Greenland. This runs for half a mile across the low heaths and then turns a couple of corners.

At the second bend you continue straight ahead, through a gate with a notice asking you to close it, which is signed by Moo. Pass the two barns and the track then goes through two iron gates. After the second the path, which is now grassy, bends to the left. There is another gate with a notice, asking you to keep the gate closed to avoid loss of cattle.

In this field there are two rights-of-way and the one you want goes to the left, diagonally across the centre, to a wooden hunting gate about 50 yards to the right of the far corner. Continue across the corner of the next field to an iron gate on to Studland Heath. Go a little to the left, but only a few feet, and then on the right you'll see a trackway uphill into the gorse. The track then crosses heather, and you aim for a point a little to the left of the belt of woodland on the horizon.

The next gate is marked "Keep this gate closed to prevent loss of cattle." You are now back inside the Nature Conservancy's Studland national nature reserve. Damp ruts are more than they seem, with insect-eating sundews and tussocks of white cotton grass. In half a mile you go straight over at a crossing of tracks and then begin the descent into an area of birch scrub. The track becomes an unmade lane, and emerges on the tarred road to the north of Studland village.

Turn right and walk back into the village, looking out for a blue sign advertising the Bankes Arms Hotel, on the left-hand side of the road. Beside it, going into the trees, there is a footpath. This brings you out in the lane leading to your car-park. Turn left and return to your car. ●

Brownsea Island trail

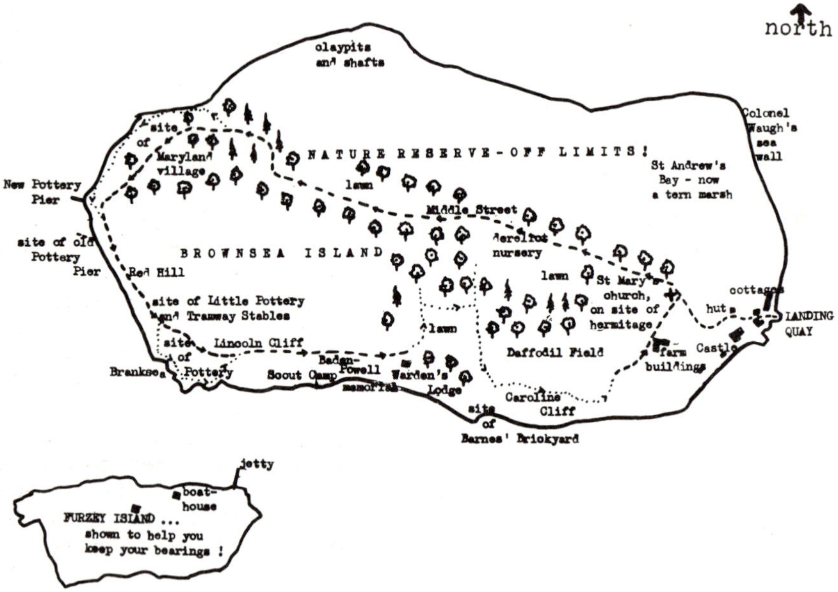

BROWNSEA ISLAND is the magic square mile of Dorset, and it is part of the Purbeck parish of Studland. It is a parable of what might happen if all the graphs of the country's decline were extrapolated into infinity. Motor cars are extinct. De-industrialisation is complete — and the island was once highly industrial, having a huge and sprawling pottery — and now the lush vegetation has smothered everything, leaving only a beach with great banks of several thousand tons of smashed sewerage pipes. There are enough of these to have drained a city. The island has even been de-agriculturalised (a phenomenon for which there does not yet exist a word). Despite having had the benefit of advice from Arthur Young, the first gardening pundit, all farming has ceased. That's the reason for offering a Brownsea walk in this issue. The absence of farm-stock means there is no reason why foot-and-mouth control area restrictions should apply to the island's paths.

The island has also been effectively depopulated, although the daytime turnover averages two thousand a week, with trips each day from the start of April to the end of September. You land at the quay, between the castle and a terrace of cottages. The castle is what you will notice, but the island's greatest engineering work, with more than a million Victorian bricks, is the sea wall to the right of the cottages. It was built to make a meadow, but has turned into a marsh. On it breeds the island tern colony. Perhaps it is still an engineering success, for there is something enduring in a bog. The other thing you may notice is that the island feels warm. Its temperature is generally about five degrees Fahrenheit higher than at Poole, the result of the long side of Brownsea being tilted towards the sun. The island is also dry, sandy and heath-covered on the southern side. This has the disadvantage of ensuring it would burn well in a drought, as it did almost from end to end in 1934, so you may well find the National Trust will close it at the peak of a hot summer.

Boats leave from Poole Quay (use a car park off the High Street, rather than hope for a space on the quay edge, as that is for short-stay use). They leave about every half hour, and take a similar length of time to reach Brownsea. Alternatively you can cross from Sandbanks, but run the risk of involving yourself in unnecessary congestion and parking difficulties. Try to turn up in the morning, or at least by lunchtime, for though the walk is only *four* miles it is full of distractions, and you'll have to be back on the island's boat-stage in time to catch the last boat at 6 p.m.

On arrival you walk across the quay to a National Trust pay kiosk. If you have not seen any notice, ask for the time of the last boat. Make sure also that you have remembered the *colour* of your ticket, because that is the boatman's way of determining whether to return you to Poole or Sandbanks. Obviously you keep the return halves of the ticket, but when a large queue surges towards a ferryboat you are unlikely to have it checked.

Walk along the gravel path. To your left is a refreshment room, with a view across to the Sandbanks—Shell Bay chain ferry. On your right are the public lavatories. The large building to the left is Brownsea Castle, which conceals beneath its 1765 shell a hexagonal gun platform of 1547. This has walls nine feet thick and was built as part of Henry VIII's coast defences — the first of any size along the English Channel since the Saxon shore forts of the Romans. It had a direct line of fire across Poole Harbour. This 16th century fort is in the basement of Humphrey Sturt's castle. He used it as the foundations for the four-storey tower, now used as a holiday home by the John Lewis Partnership. It is not opened to the public, but you can at the time of writing peer through a gap in the hedge. The space should be left. If general access to the castle is not possible, there should at least be an opportunity for a harmless peep.

The path then passes the edge of the tern marsh, the hundred acres added to the island by Colonel William Waugh in 1853. It lies beyond the belt of sallow scrub to the right of the path, and again you have to be content with glimpses. There is a Dorset Naturalists' Trust information post and hide, with details about conducted walks through their reserve on the island, which has only restricted access. By all means join their trail instead of ours if you happen to be around at the right time. You'll see the heronry and the island's two large lakes, and stand a better chance of spotting the island's special rarity, the red squirrel. It survives because the greys have not been introduced to the island.

To your left there is a wide sweep of grass, with an abundance of peafowl. Picking up peacock feathers is an island taboo, because some visitors who fail to find any start plucking them from the birds. The church was also built by Waugh in 1853, and cost him £10,000 (almost as much as he paid for the island, £13,000 in 1852). He had been told that the island contained "the finest clay" worth "at a low computation, at least £100,000 an acre". On the strength of that he raised £237,000 from the London and Eastern Banking Corporation, of which he was a director, and built the Branksea Pottery and Clay Works at the other end of the island.

The church is St.Mary's, but on its site was an ancient chapel and hermitage, built by the monks of Cerne Abbas. It was dedicated to St. Andrew, with St.Andrew's Bay being the name of the tern marsh before it was drained. The present church is a monument to the rich living of Brownsea's Victorian and Edwardian owners, with an effigy of Charles van Raalte. G.Augustus Cavendish-Bentinck, who owned the island from 1870 to 1890, brought over the 17th century iron well-head from Italy. It marks his grave. The earlier chapel is worth remembering, for it is recorded as the only building on the island when King Canute landed on Brownsea in 1015. Something was left of it when Waugh built his church, for he took "particular care to preserve the small portion of the chapel wall which remains". If you can find this, write to us!

The walk proceeds along the north side of the church, away from the peacock lawns and into the trees. This older belt of scrubland is the coolest part of the island, being damp and shaded. Pink rhododendrons, the weed of the Dorset heaths, proliferate. This is Middle Street and the track passes another patch of open grass, and the derelict brick ruins of the former nursery garden. The track continues in a more or less straight line for more than half a mile. You pass another

1793 print of Brownsea Castle, from the lavishly illustrated but unobtainable Second Edition of John Hutchins's County History. Courtesy: Dorset County Magazine

length of grass, kept short by tractors rather than the wildlife, and a fire lookout. All the gates to the right of the path are locked as they lead into the nature reserve, which apart from its conducted tours is off-limits to ordinary visitors.

At the end of the long stretch of grass the track bends to the right and passes through dense pine woods. There are usually some extremely large and active ant-hills. You can either take the main path, or strike off to the right on one of the narrow tracks through the rhododendron bushes. These tracks bring you down on to the beach, and you turn left along it. Look out for shelduck nests, which will probably have been tagged by the warden.

This part of the island is called Maryland and was the site of an impressive crescent of pottery workers' cottages. A horsedrawn tramway passed between the cottages and the shore and headed off into what is now the nature reserve to claypits and underground mines at Seymer's Marsh. The main track reaches the water at Pottery Pier, which has been reconstructed on a modest scale for private yachts.

The path continues to the south, to Red Hill and Lincoln Cliff. From this corner of the island you look across to the backwaters of Poole Harbour and Arne peninsula. Corfe Castle shows up on its mound at the break in the line of the Purbeck Hills. The three islands in the near distance are (from left to right) Furzey Island, Green Island and Round Island. The first two are close and appear to merge together. Make sure you venture on to the beach somewhere along this stretch. It is strewn with thousands of tons of stoneware pipes, up to eight feet high, on the shore opposite the

Humphrey Sturt's castle and the Brownsea Road anchorage, from another contemporary print
Courtesy: Wimborne Bookshop

right-hand end of Furzey Island. There are also vitrified bricks, from the linings of the island's many kilns.

You come to an expanse of grassland, directly opposite the boathouse at the centre of Furzey Island. Foundations of the main pottery buildings, which had a tall chimney, can be seen as bumps and hollows across the grass. The chimney was the great landmark of Poole Harbour, a century before Hamworthy power station.

Next the main track passes the Scout Camp, which apart from being one of the most perfect places for a camp also has an abundance of sentimental associations. On the ridge after the camp there is a memorial to Robert Baden-Powell's first scout camp, set up near here in the southwest part of Brownsea in 1907.

You pass the Warden's Lodge and come out on a large square of grassland. It is best to walk to the left and follow this around the inland edge, because on the far side there are two beautiful glades leading into the trees. One, at the first corner, is Swindale, and the other, Rocket Corner with a little pool, leads off from the next corner.

If you continue following the edge of the trees you skirt Harley Wood and come into the Daffodil Field. Follow this field around its seaward extremity, looking across to Little Sea and Studland. The mild conditions are ideal for the young strawberry trees that are growing amongst the scrub oak of the cliffside, and this is one of the few places where they grow wild in Britain. Their principal toehold, also by the sea, is beside the fiords in the south-west corner of Ireland.

The track back is now well signposted, and you come to the sloping lawns above the church. The buildings to your right are those of the island's 19th century farm. The track brings you down to the church and you turn right, returning to the quay and the ferry. ●

St Mary's Church, Brownsea, in its Victorian halcyon days, engraved by Philip Brannon
Courtesy: Dorset County Magazine